FOR ORGANS, PIANOS & ELECTRONIC KEYBOARDS

E-Z PLAY TODAY

10

Songs of HAWAII

Cover photo courtesy Library of Congress, Prints & Photographs Division
Photograph by Carol M. Highsmith

ISBN 978-1-4950-7614-5

7777 W. BLUEMOUND RD. P.O. BOX 13819 MILWAUKEE, WI 53213

E-Z Play® TODAY Music Notation © 1975 HAL LEONARD LLC
E-Z PLAY and EASY ELECTRONIC KEYBOARD MUSIC are registered trademarks of HAL LEONARD LLC.

Visit Hal Leonard Online at
www.halleonard.com

Aloha Nui Kuu Ipo

Registration 1
Rhythm: Ballad or Fox Trot

Words and Music by
Alvin Isaacs

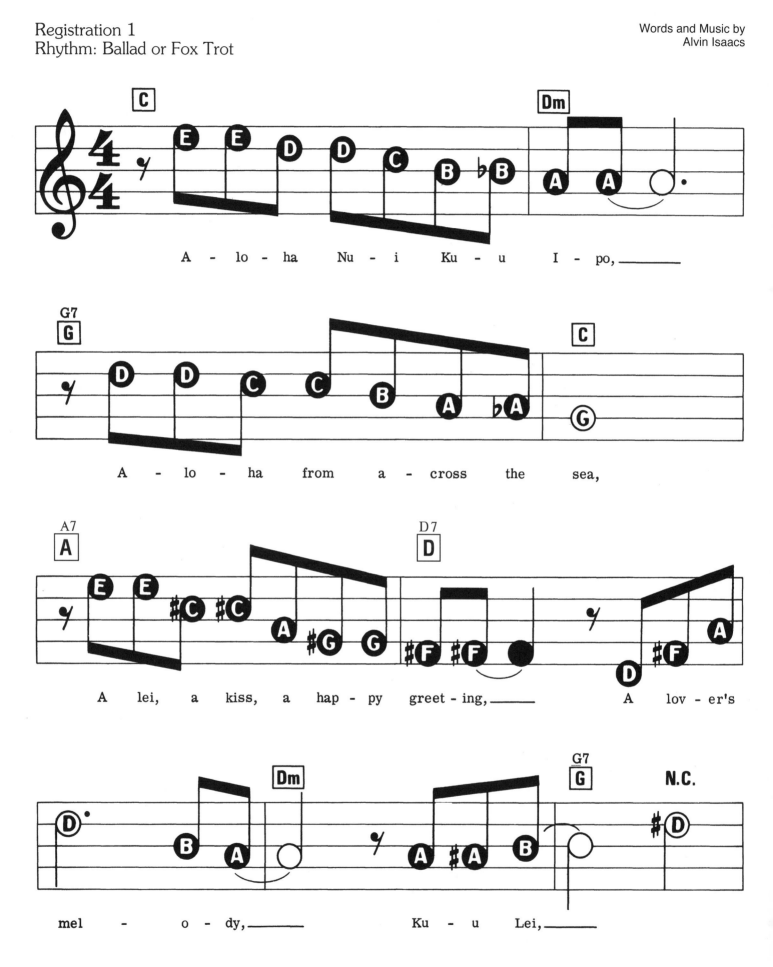

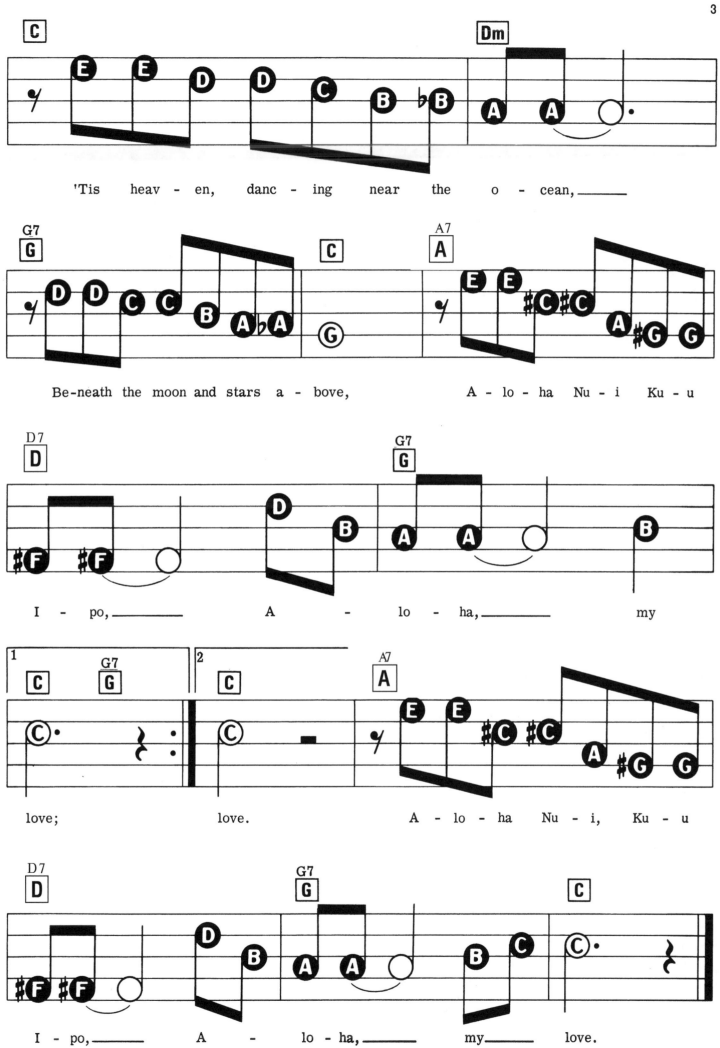

Aloha Oe

Registration 2
Rhythm: Swing

Words and Music by
Queen Liliuokalani

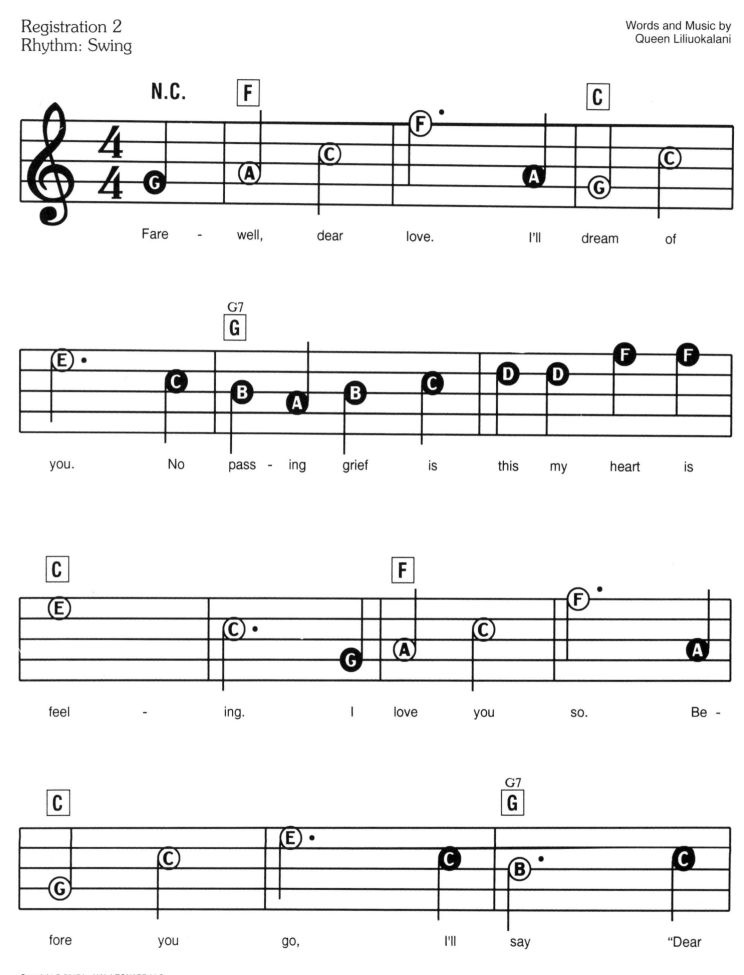

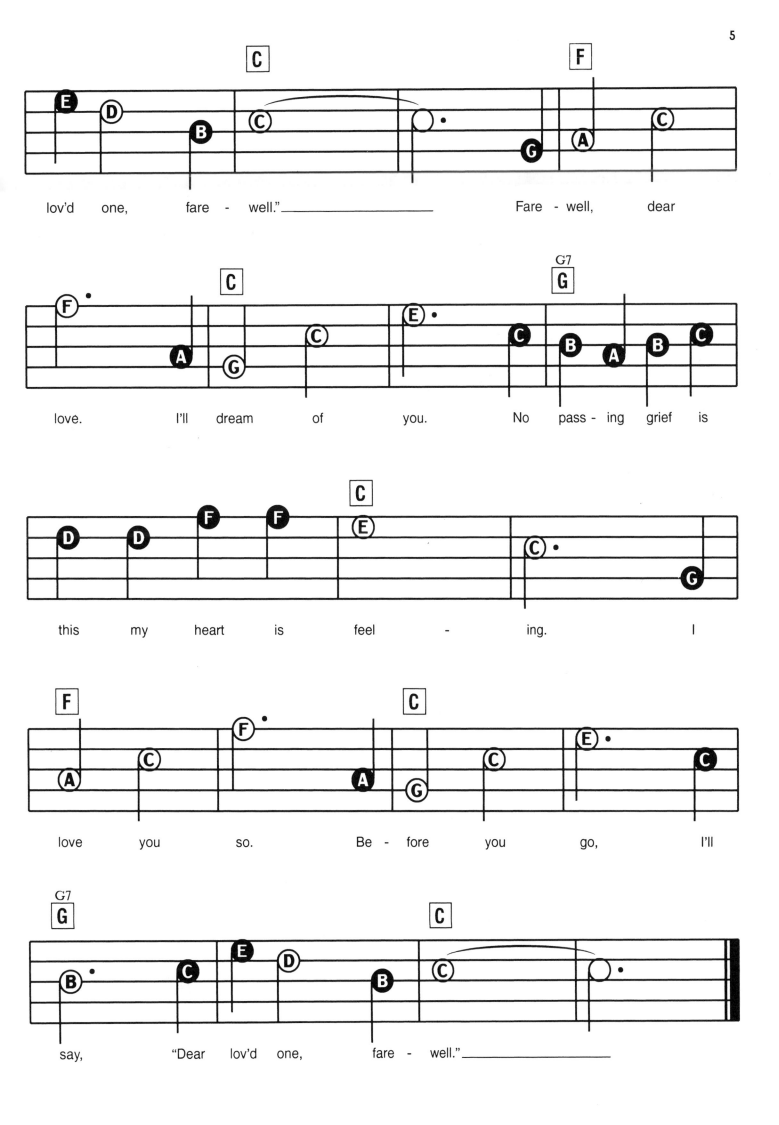

Beautiful Kahana

Registration 4
Rhythm: Ballad or None

Words by Mary J. Montano
Music by Charles E. King

For - ev - er I shall sing _____ the _____
o - la, un - ex -

prais - es of Ka - ha - na's beau - ty un - sur -
celled _____ in _____ gran - deur, stands for - ev - er

passed. The fra - grance of the beau - teous _____
near thee. For thou art en - dowed with spe - cial _____

moun - tains by the zeph - yrs to _____ thee is
charms _____ and _____ fa - vored with a place by the

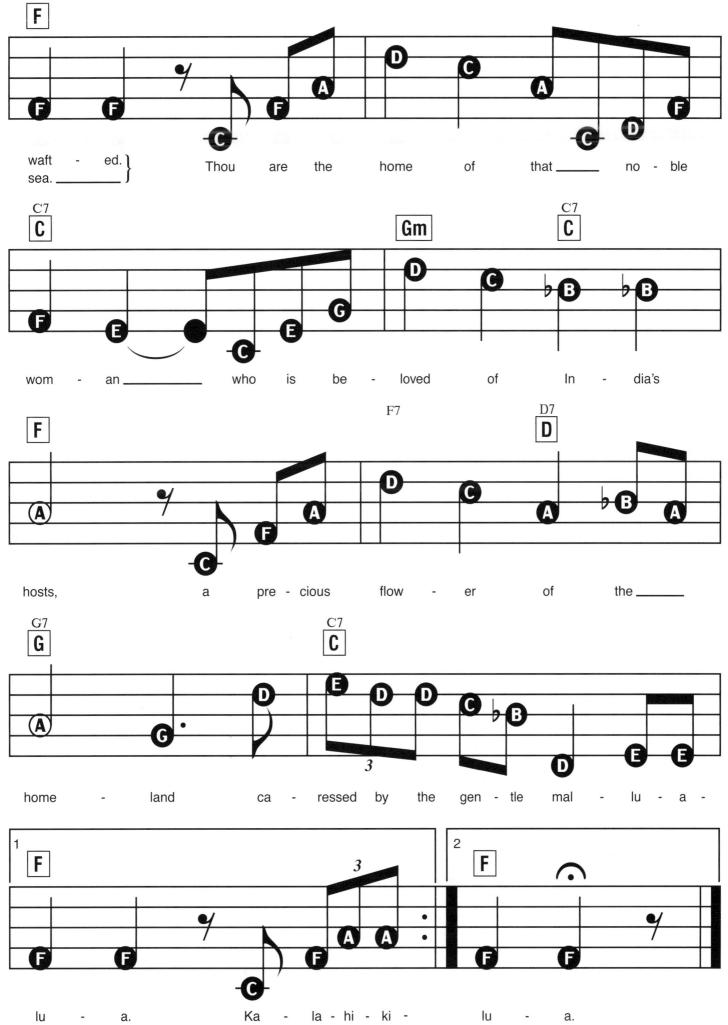

Beyond the Reef

Registration 5
Rhythm: Fox Trot or Swing

Words and Music by
Jack Pitman

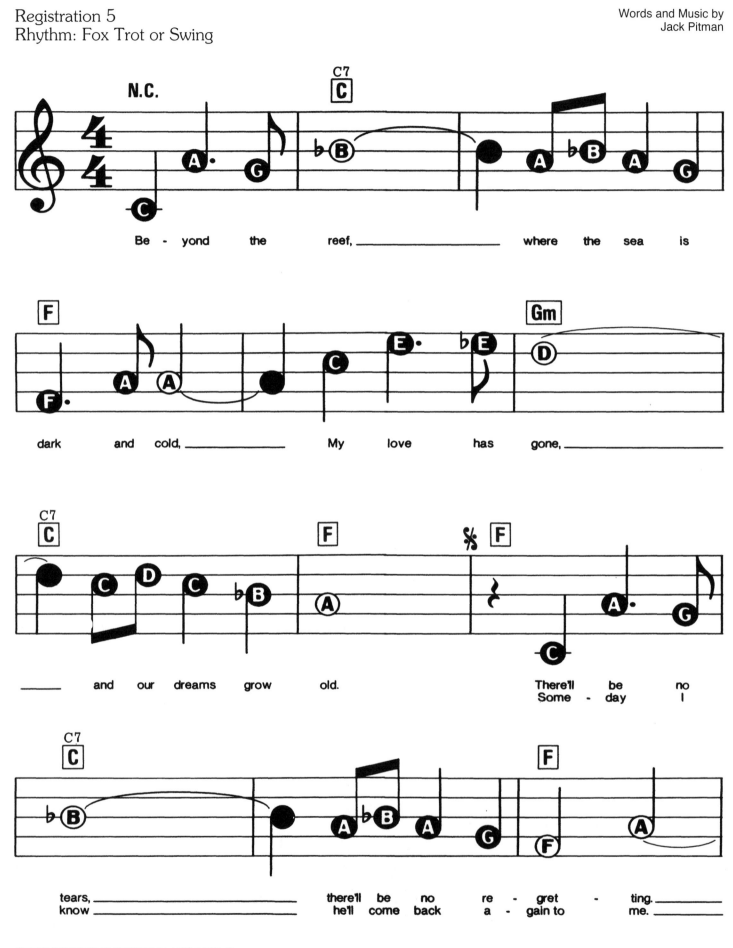

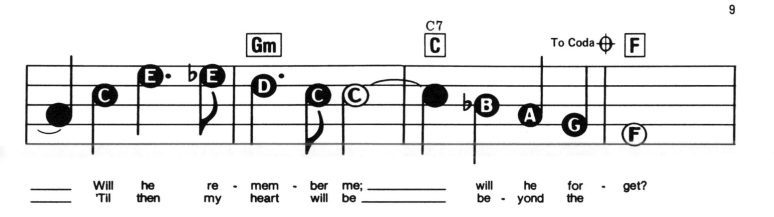

_____ Will he re-mem-ber me; _____ will he for-get?
_____ 'Til then my heart will be _____ be-yond the

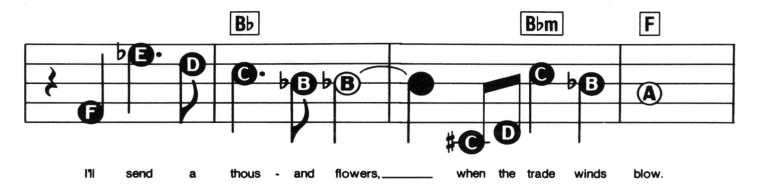

I'll send a thous-and flowers,_____ when the trade winds blow.

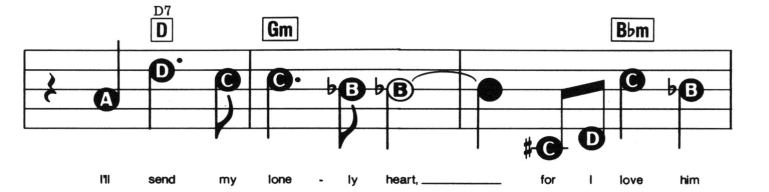

I'll send my lone-ly heart,_____ for I love him

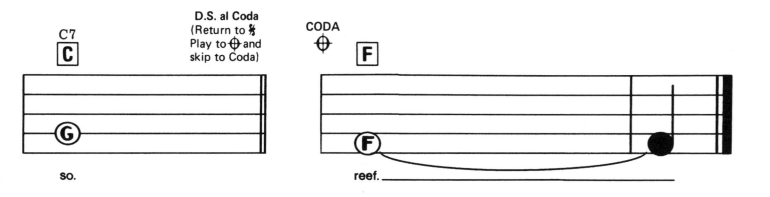

so.   reef. _____

Blue Hawaii
from the Paramount Picture WAIKIKI WEDDING

Registration 7
Rhythm: Fox Trot or Pops

Words and Music by Leo Robin
and Ralph Rainger

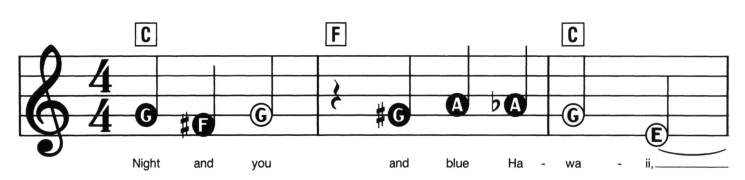

Night and you and blue Ha - wa - ii,

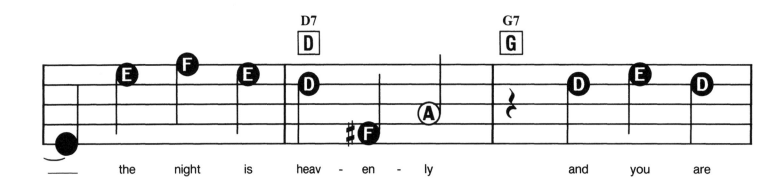

the night is heav - en - ly and you are

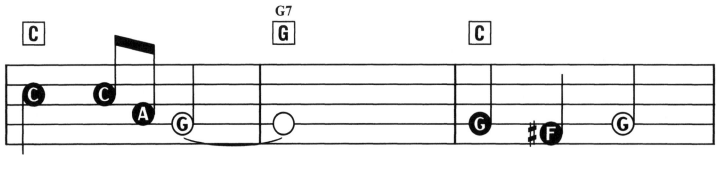

heav - en to me. Love - ly you

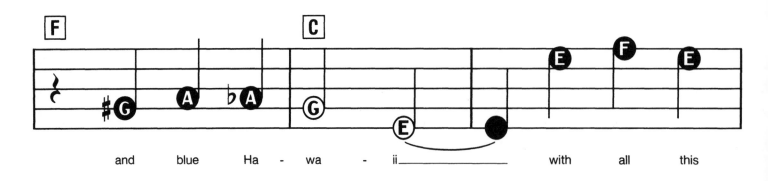

and blue Ha - wa - ii with all this

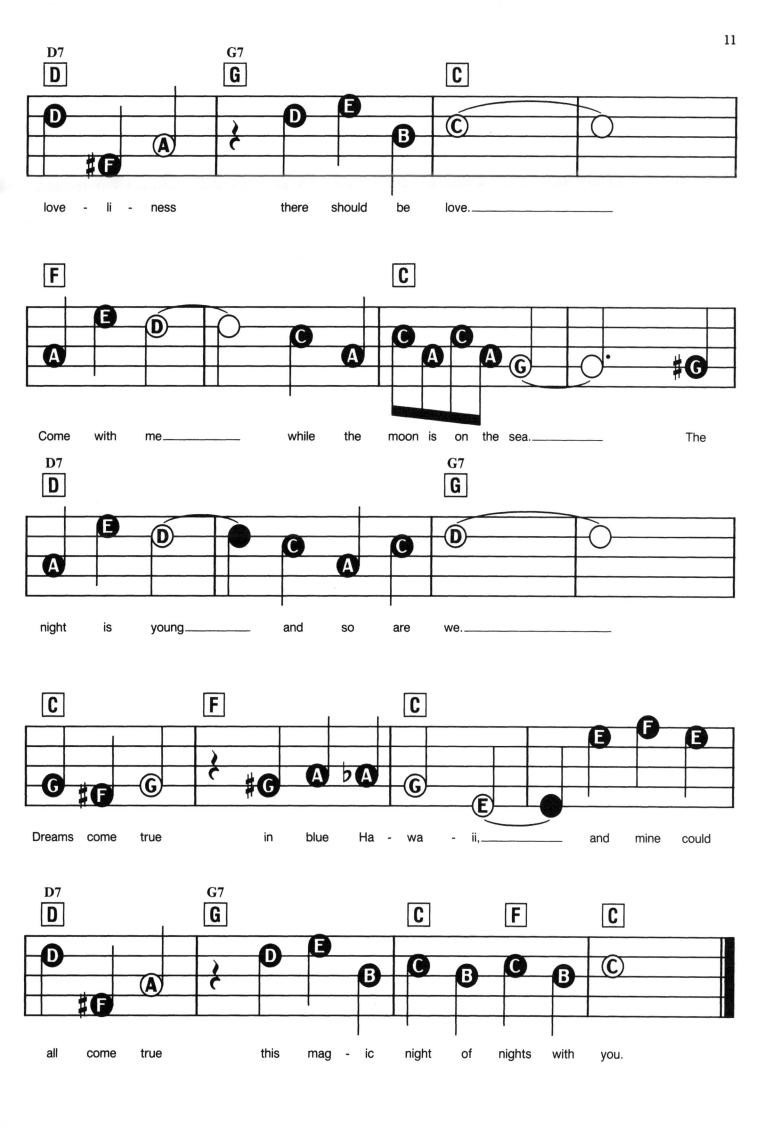

Drifting and Dreaming
(Sweet Paradise)

Registration 2
Rhythm: Fox Trot or Swing

Words by Haven Gillespie
Music by Egbert Van Alstyne,
Erwin R. Schmidt and Loyal Curtis

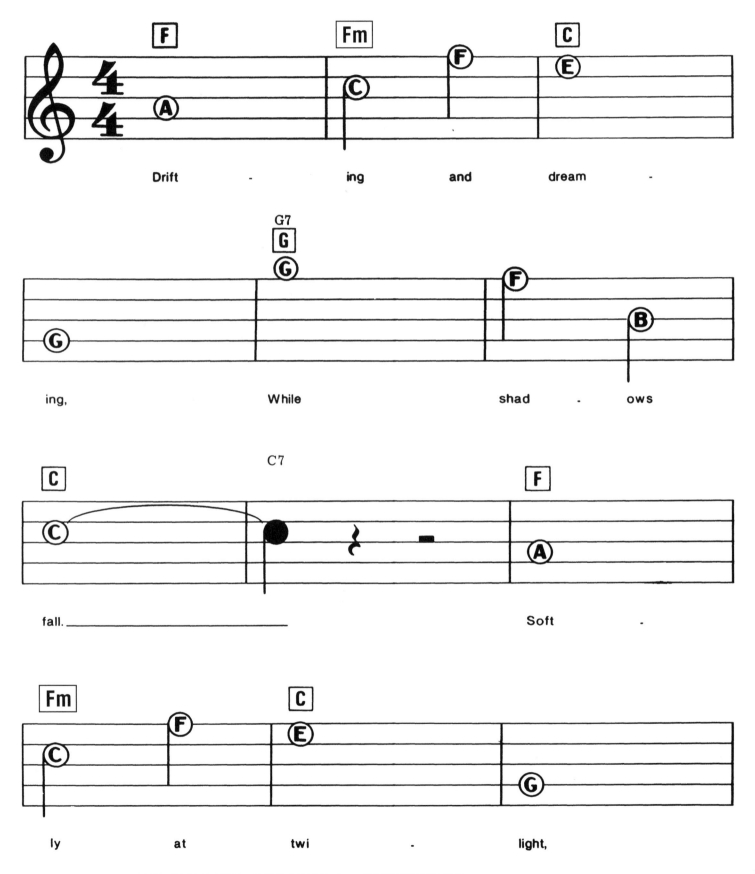

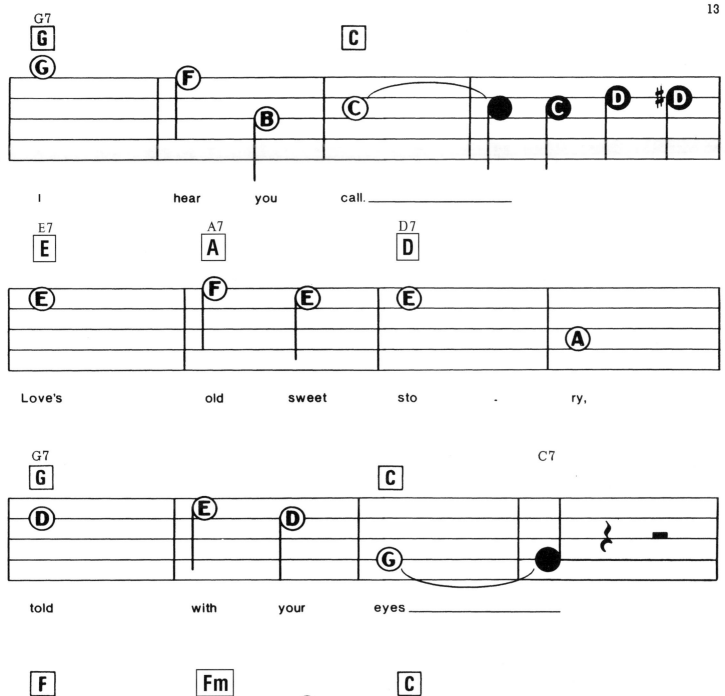

I   hear   you   call. _____

Love's   old   sweet   sto - ry,

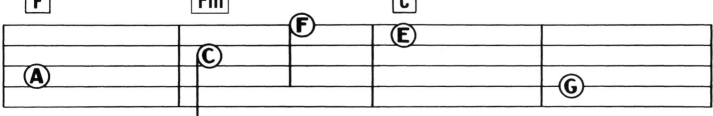

told   with   your   eyes _____

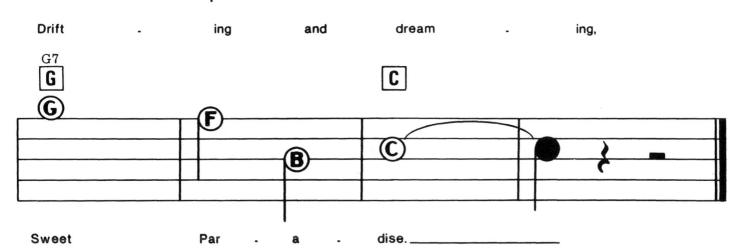

Drift - ing   and   dream - ing,

Sweet   Par . a . dise. _____

Hanalei Moon

Registration 4
Rhythm: Ballad or Fox Trot

Words and Music by
Bob Nelson

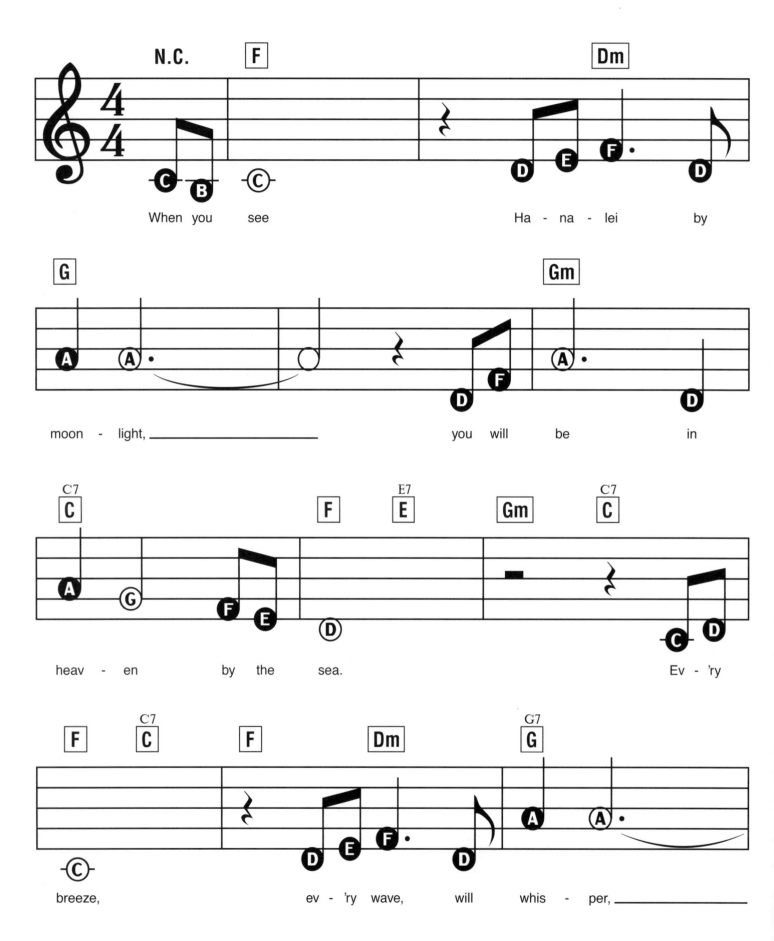

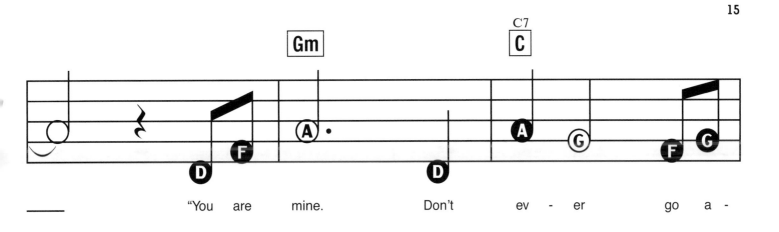

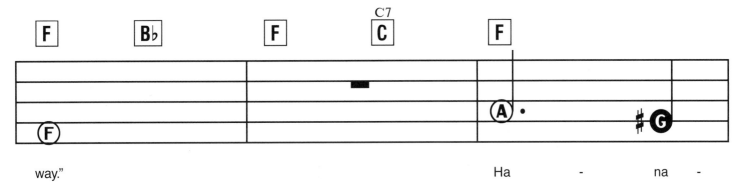

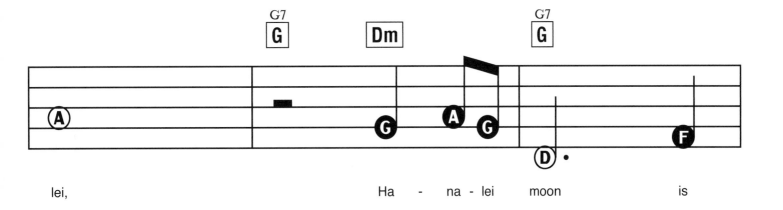

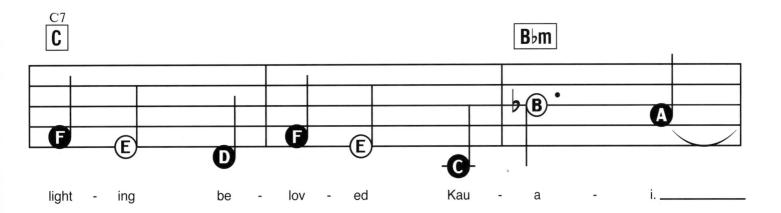

15

_____ "You are mine. Don't ev - er go a -

way." Ha - na -

lei, Ha - na - lei moon is

light - ing be - lov - ed Kau - a - i. _____

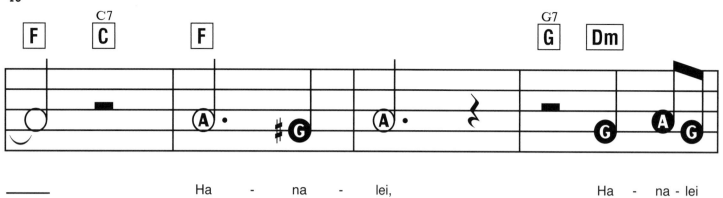

Ha - na - lei,   Ha - na - lei

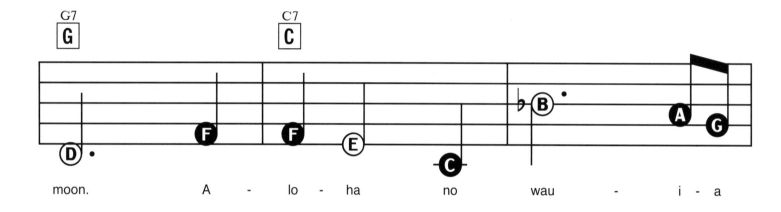

moon.   A - lo - ha   no   wau - i - a

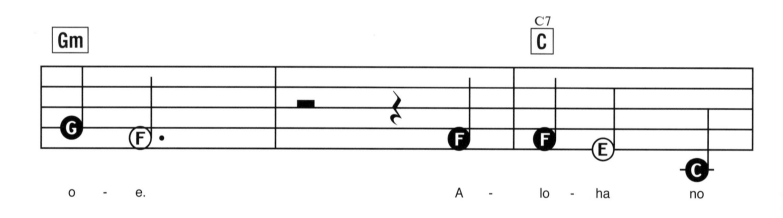

o - e.   A - lo - ha   no

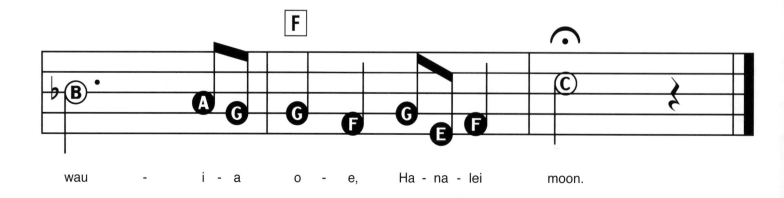

wau - i - a   o - e,   Ha - na - lei   moon.

Hawaii Ponoi

Registration 2
Rhythm: Waltz

Words and Music by King Kalakaua
and Henri Berger

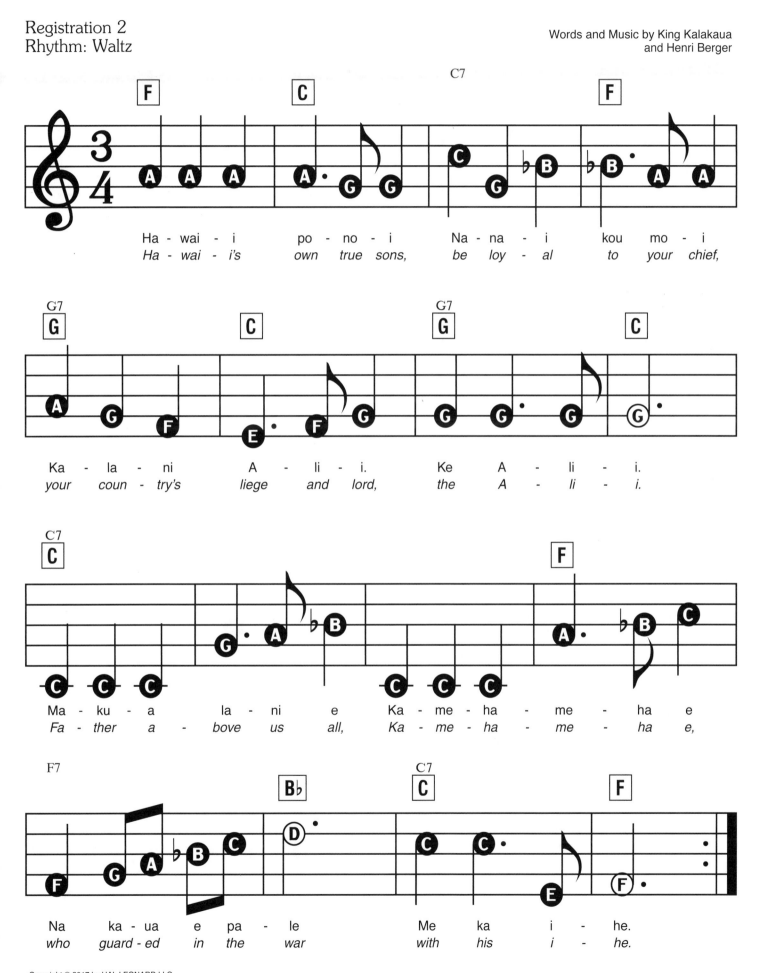

Hawaiian Love Call

Registration 1
Rhythm: Fox Trot

Written by
Aluli Irmgard Farden

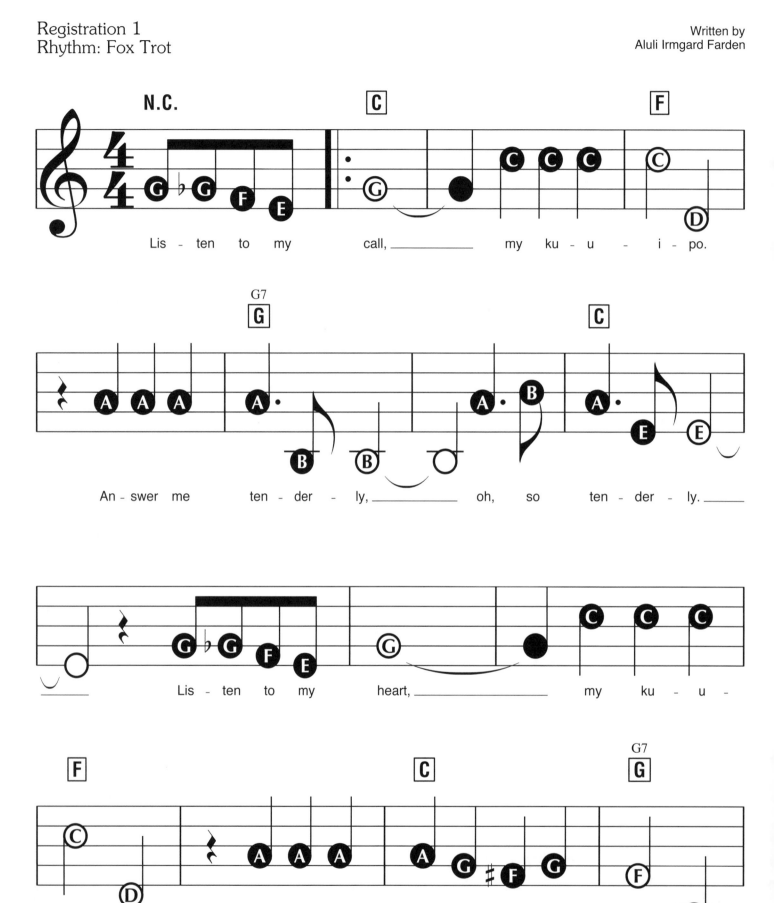

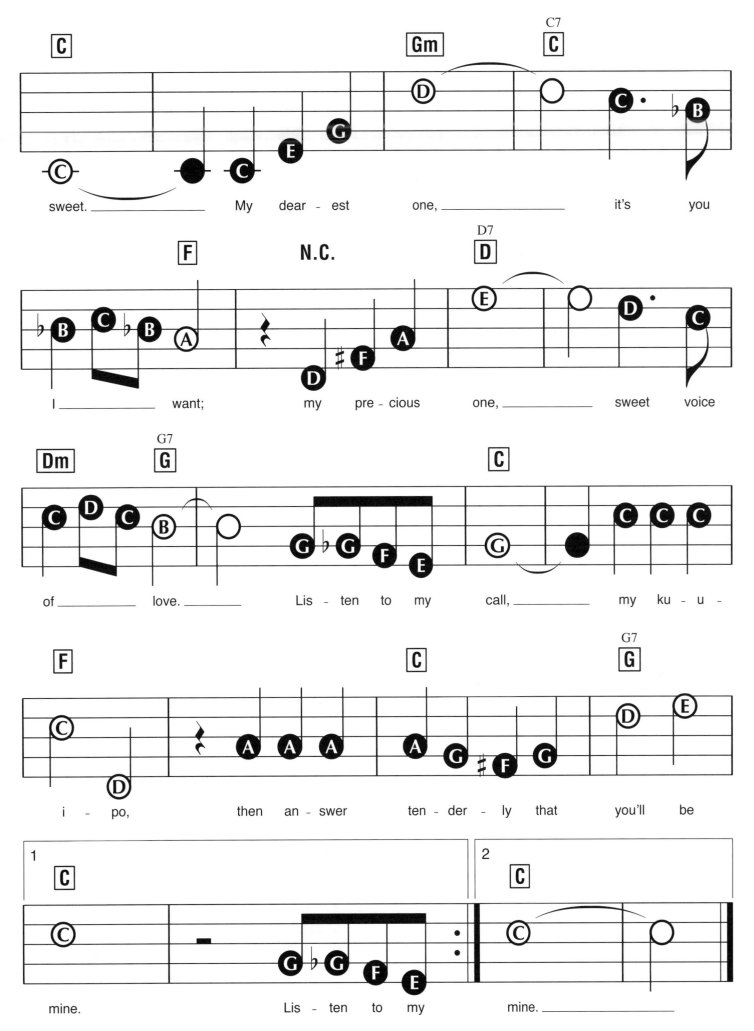

Hawaiian Roller Coaster Ride
from *LILO & STITCH*

Registration 2
Rhythm: None

Words and Music by Alan Silvestri
and Mark Keali'i Ho'omalu

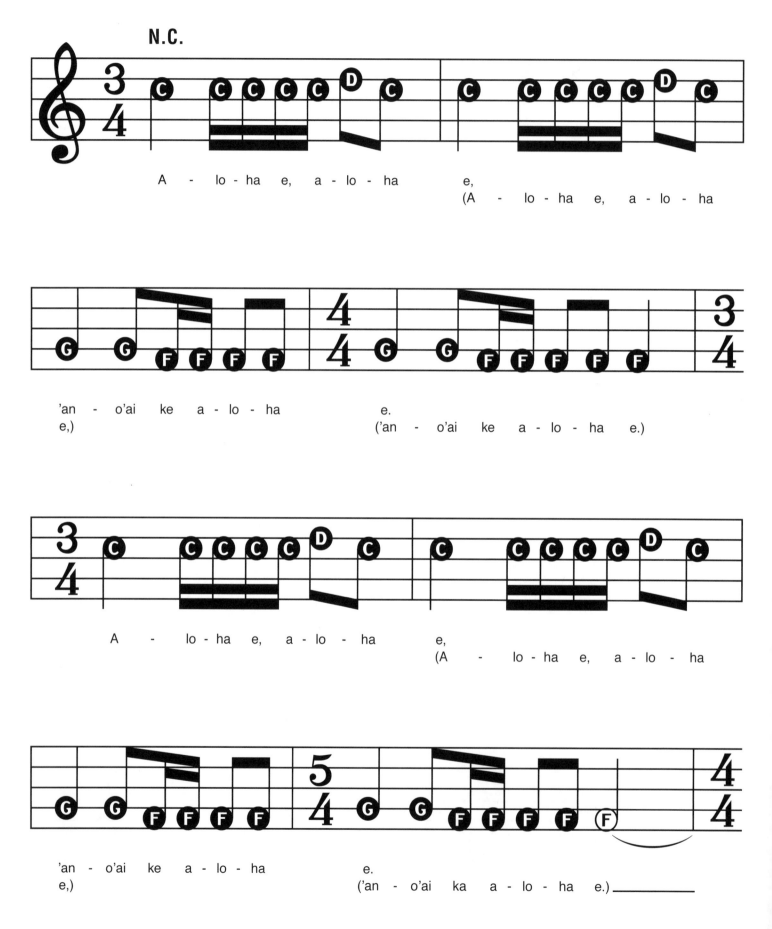

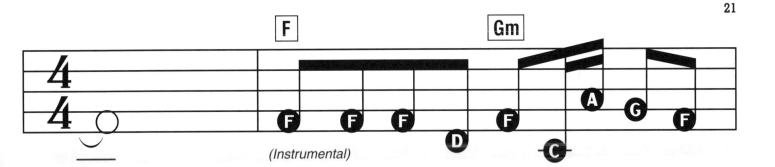

(Instrumental)

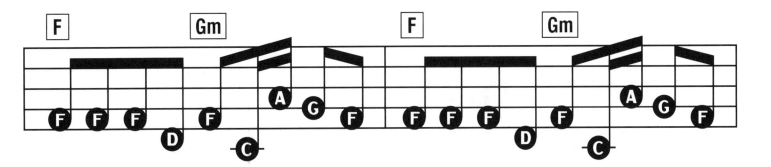

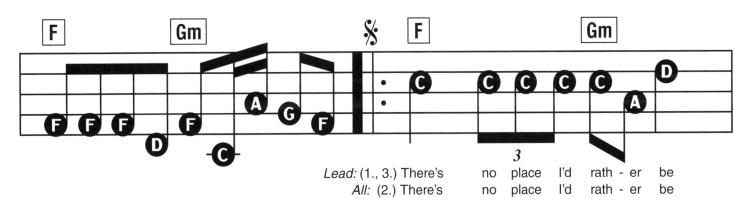

Lead: (1., 3.) There's no place I'd rath-er be
All: (2.) There's no place I'd rath-er be

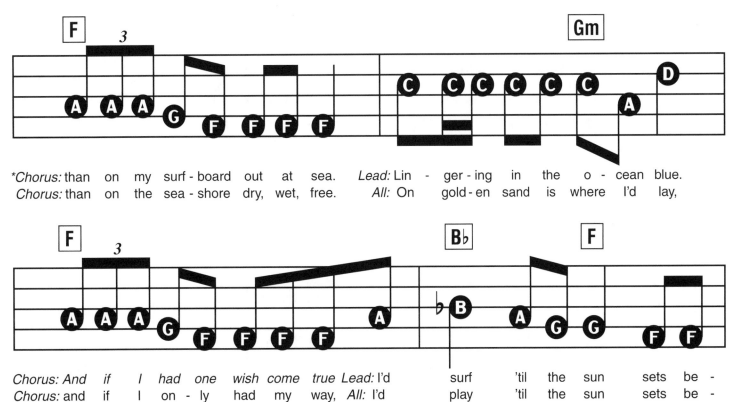

*Chorus: than on my surf-board out at sea. Lead: Lin-ger-ing in the o-cean blue.
Chorus: than on the sea-shore dry, wet, free. All: On gold-en sand is where I'd lay,

Chorus: And if I had one wish come true Lead: I'd surf 'til the sun sets be -
Chorus: and if I on-ly had my way, All: I'd play 'til the sun sets be -

* Childrens' chorus

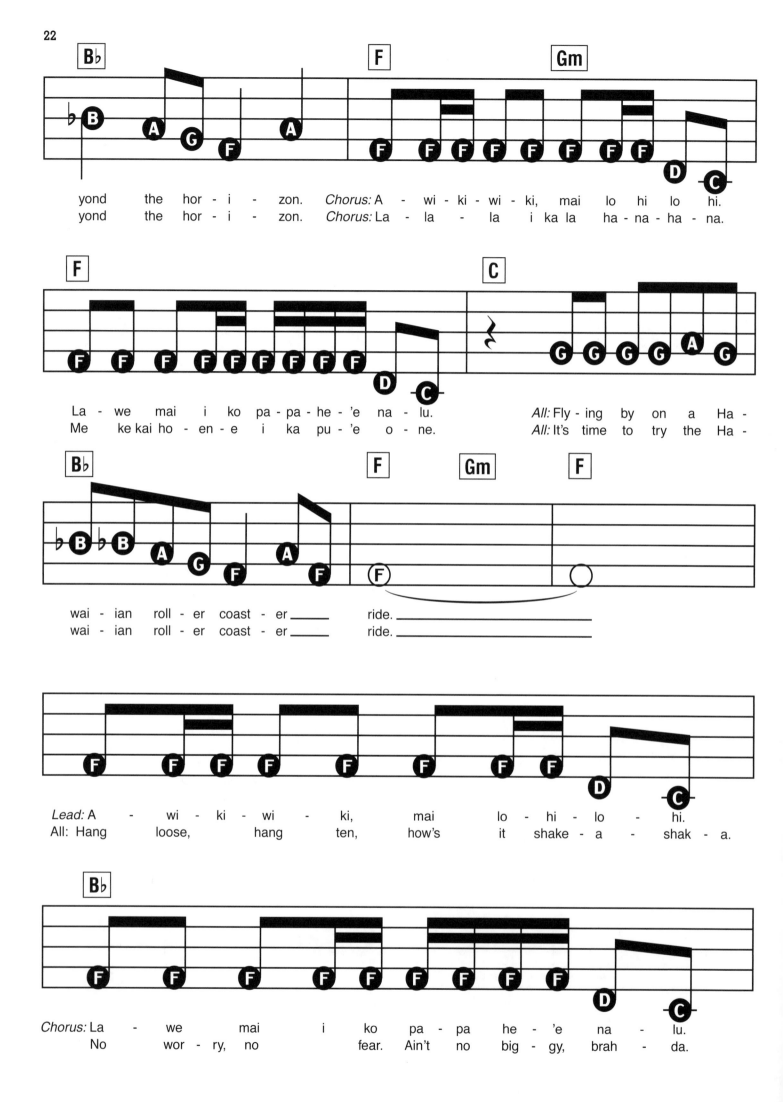

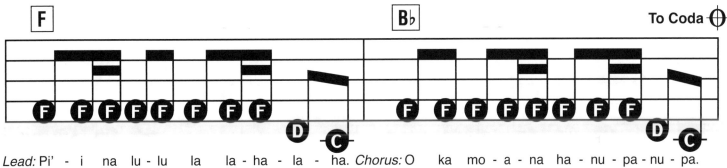

F   **B♭**   **To Coda** ⊕

Lead: Pi' - i na lu-lu la la-ha-la-ha.   *Chorus:* O ka mo-a-na ha-nu-pa-nu-pa.

Put-tin' in, cut-tin' up, cut-tin' back, cut-tin'out,   Front side, back side, goof-y-foot-ed wipe out.

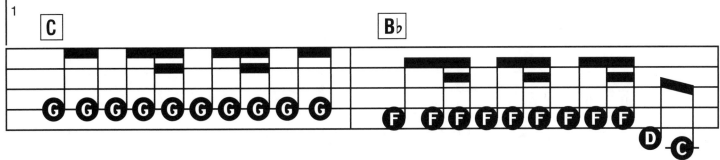

1   **C**   **B♭**

Lead: La - la - la i ka la ha - na - ha - na.   *Chorus:* Me ke kai ho - en - e i ka pu - 'e one.

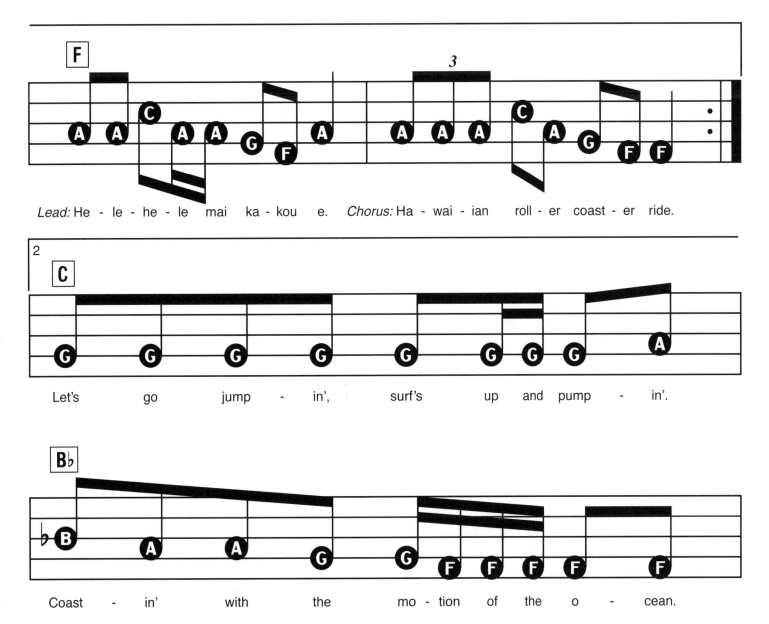

F   *3*

Lead: He - le - he - le mai ka - kou e.   *Chorus:* Ha - wai - ian roll - er coast - er ride.

2   **C**

Let's go jump - in', surf's up and pump - in'.

B♭

Coast - in' with the mo - tion of the o - cean.

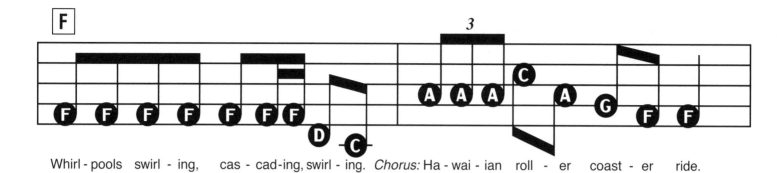

Whirl - pools swirl - ing, cas - cad-ing, swirl - ing. *Chorus:* Ha - wai - ian roll - er coast - er ride.

D.S. al Coda
(Return to %
Play to ⊕ and
Skip to Coda)

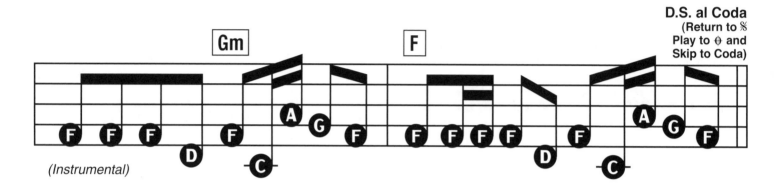

(Instrumental)

CODA

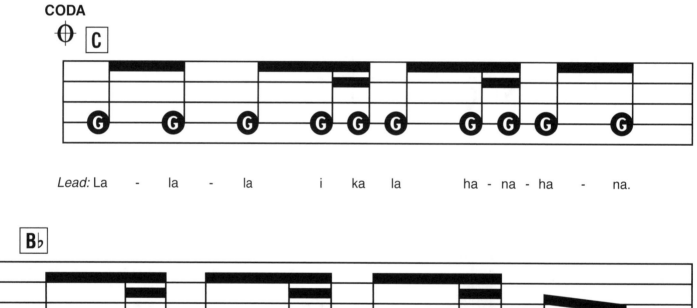

Lead: La - la - la i ka la ha - na - ha - na.

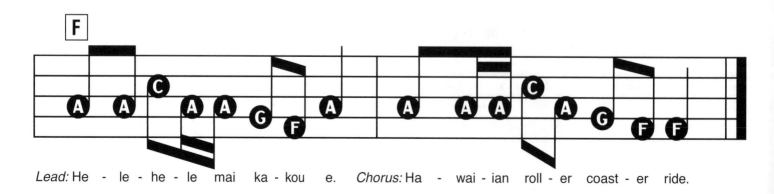

Chorus: Me ke kai ho - en - e i ka pu - 'e one.

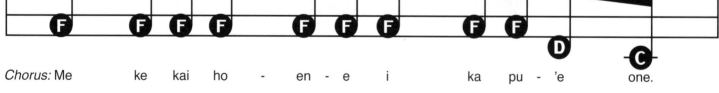

Lead: He - le - he - le mai ka - kou e. *Chorus:* Ha - wai - ian roll - er coast - er ride.

Hawaiian War Chant
(Ta-Hu-Wa-Hu-Wai)

Registration 5
Rhythm: Swing

English Lyrics by Ralph Freed
Music by Johnny Noble and Leleiohaku

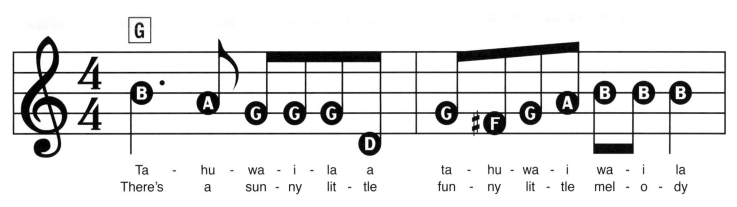

Ta - hu - wa - i - la   a   ta - hu - wa - i   wa - i   la
There's   a   sun - ny   lit - tle   fun - ny   lit - tle   mel - o - dy

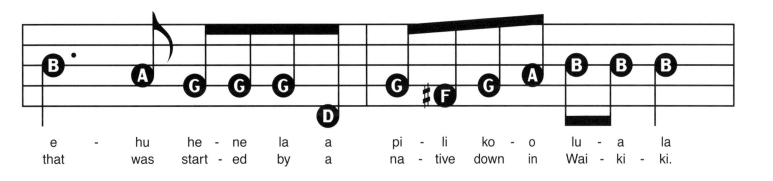

e - hu   he - ne   la   a   pi - li   ko - o   lu - a   la
that   was   start - ed   by   a   na - tive   down   in   Wai - ki - ki.

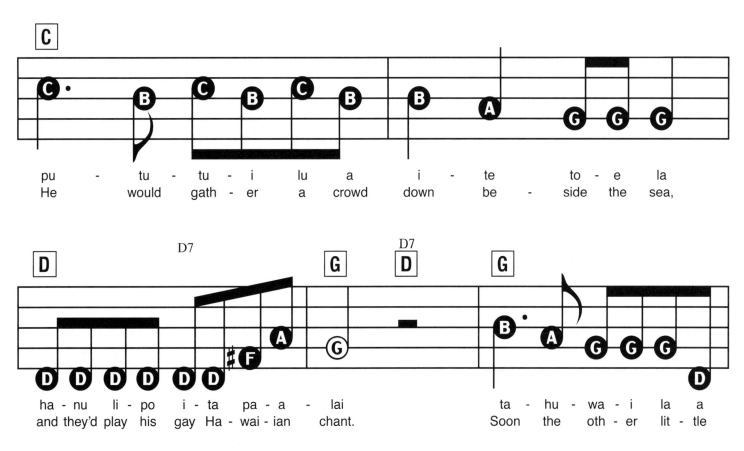

pu - tu - tu - i   lu   a   i - te   to - e   la
He   would   gath - er   a   crowd   down   be - side   the   sea,

ha - nu   li - po   i - ta   pa - a - lai   ta - hu - wa - i   la   a
and   they'd   play   his   gay   Ha - wai - ian   chant.   Soon   the   oth - er   lit - tle

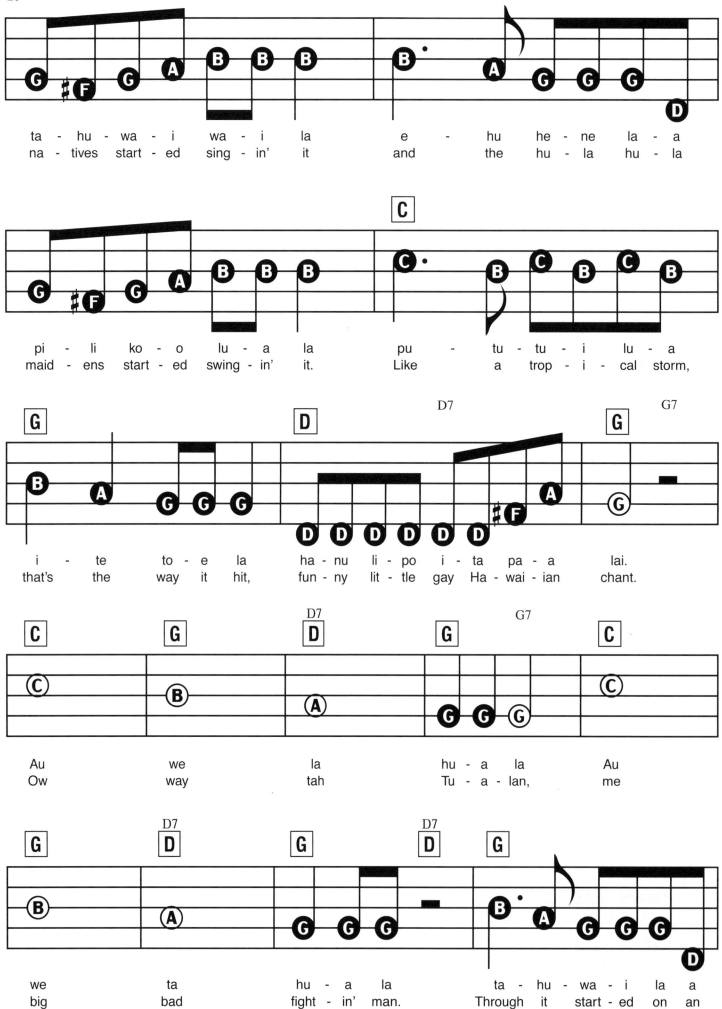

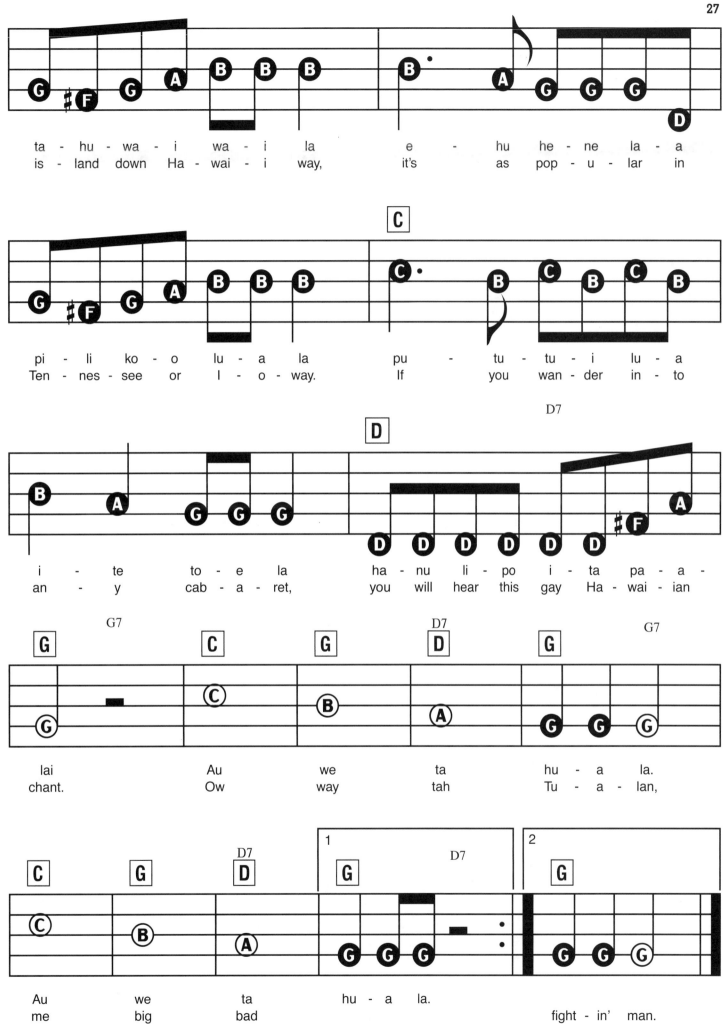

The Hawaiian Wedding Song
(Ke Kali Nei Au)

Registration 1
Rhythm: Ballad or Fox Trot

English Lyrics by Al Hoffman and Dick Manning
Hawaiian Lyrics and Music by Charles E. King

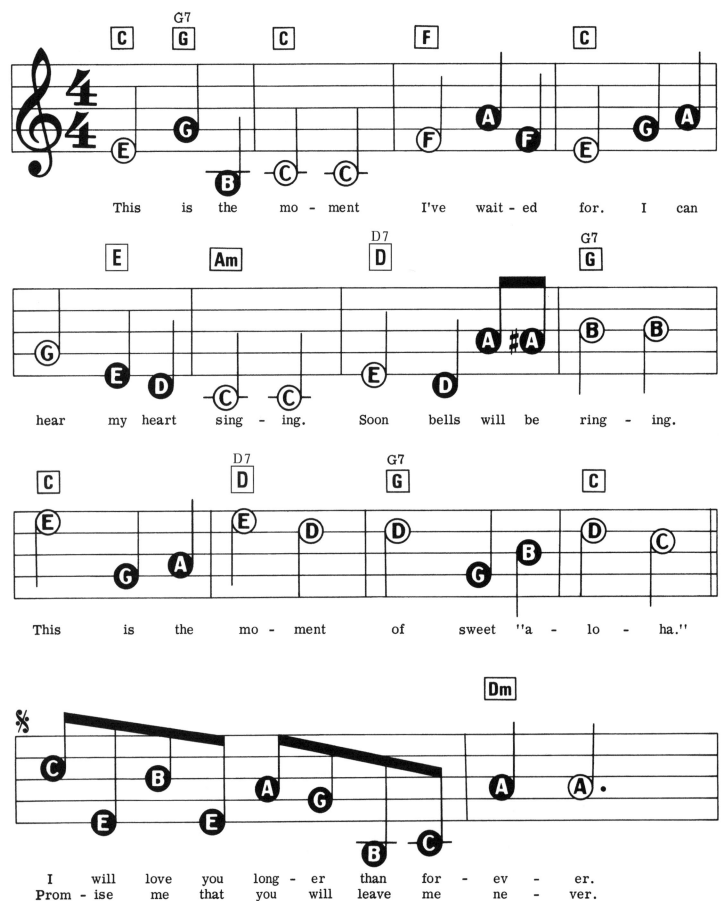

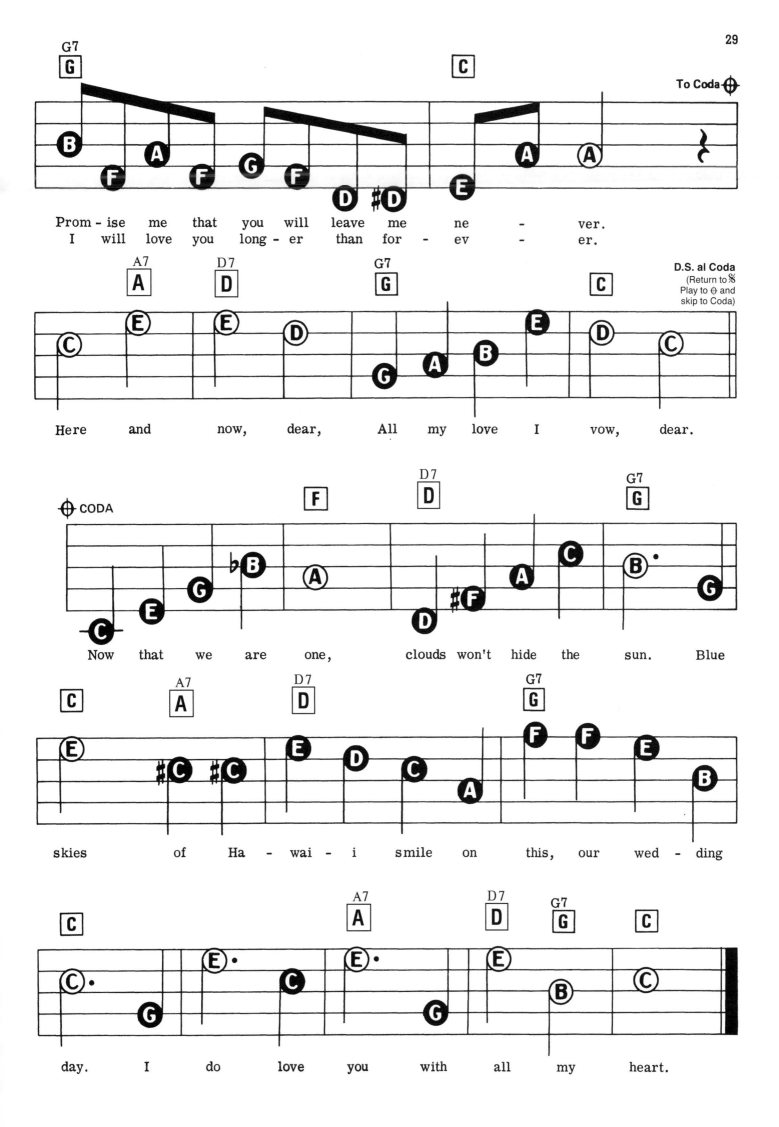

Hi'ilawe

Registration 4
Rhythm: Ballad

Words and Music by
Sam Li'a Kalainaina Sr.

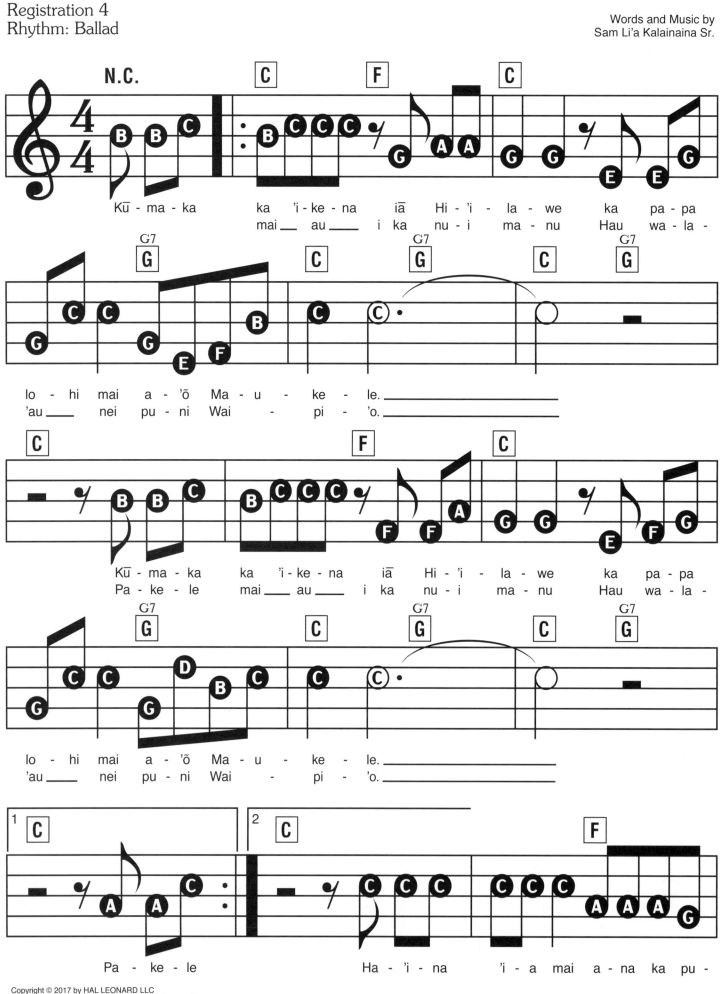

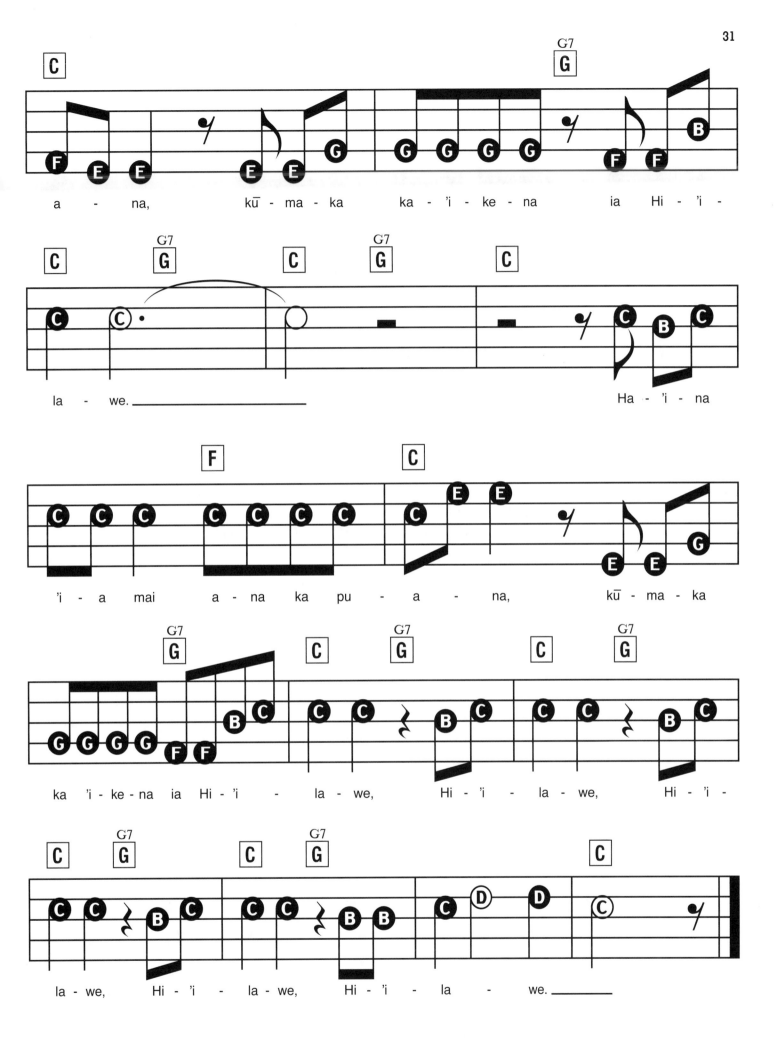

English translation
All eyes are on Hi'ilawe and the sparkling lowlands of Maukele.
I escape all the birds chattering everywhere in Waipi'o.
Tell the refrain: All eyes are on Hi'ilawe.

I'll Remember You

Registration 8
Rhythm: Ballad

Words and Music by
Kuiokalani Lee

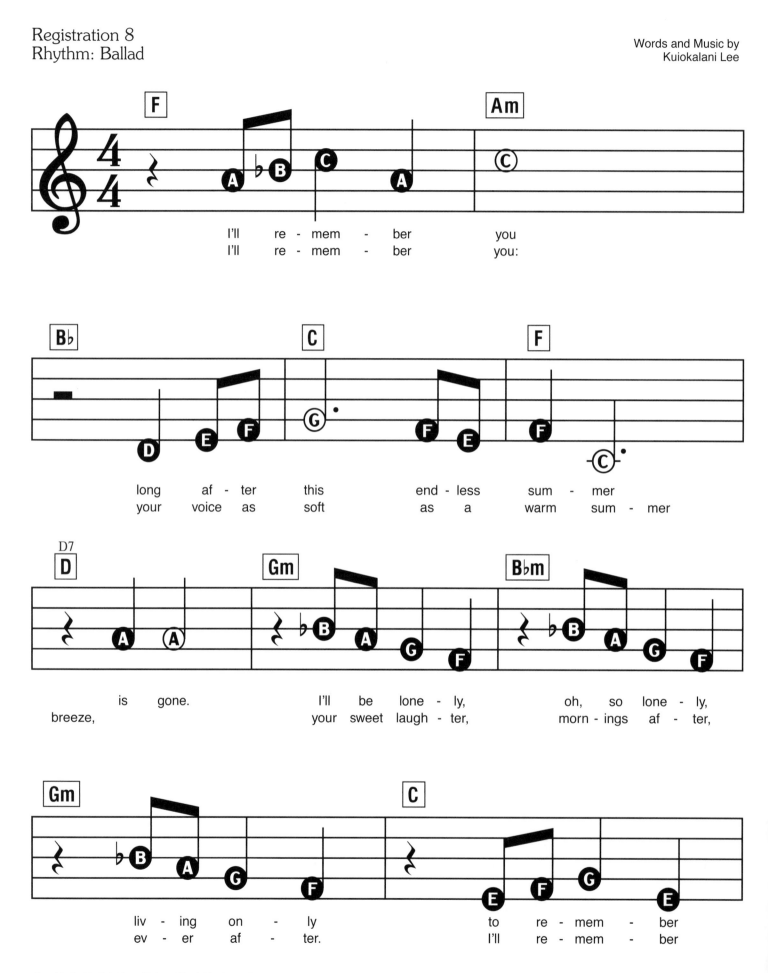

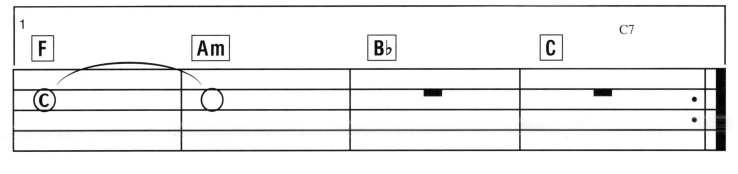

you. _____

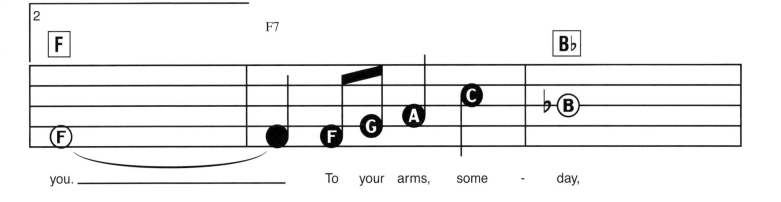

you. _____ To your arms, some - day,

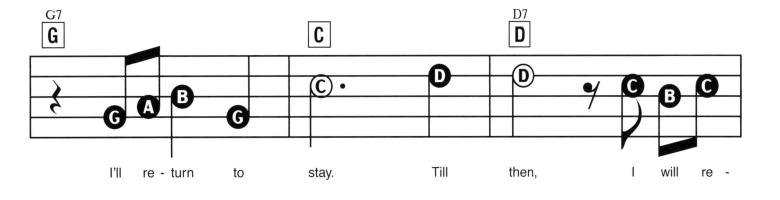

I'll re - turn to stay. Till then, I will re -

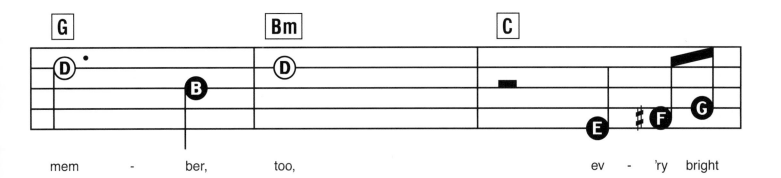

mem - ber, too, ev - 'ry bright

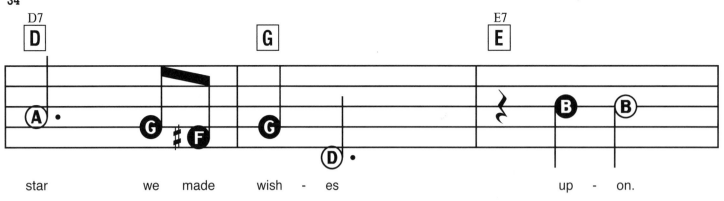

star   we   made   wish - es   up - on.

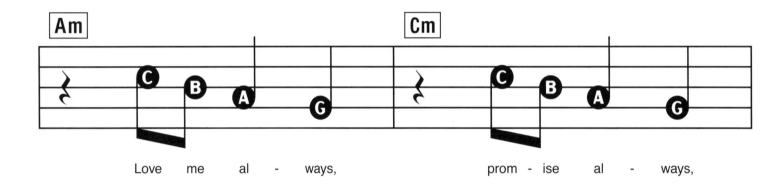

Love   me   al - ways,   prom - ise   al - ways,

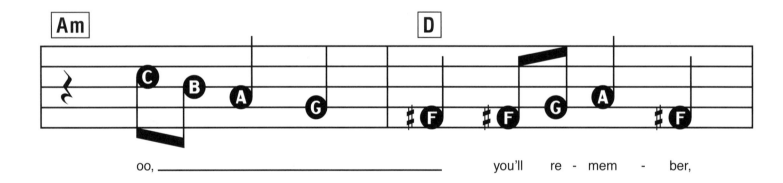

oo, _____   you'll   re - mem - ber,

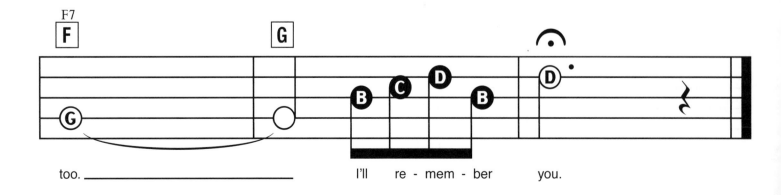

too. _____   I'll   re - mem - ber   you.

Mapuana

Registration 4
Rhythm: Ballad or 8-Beat

Words and Music by
Lani Sang

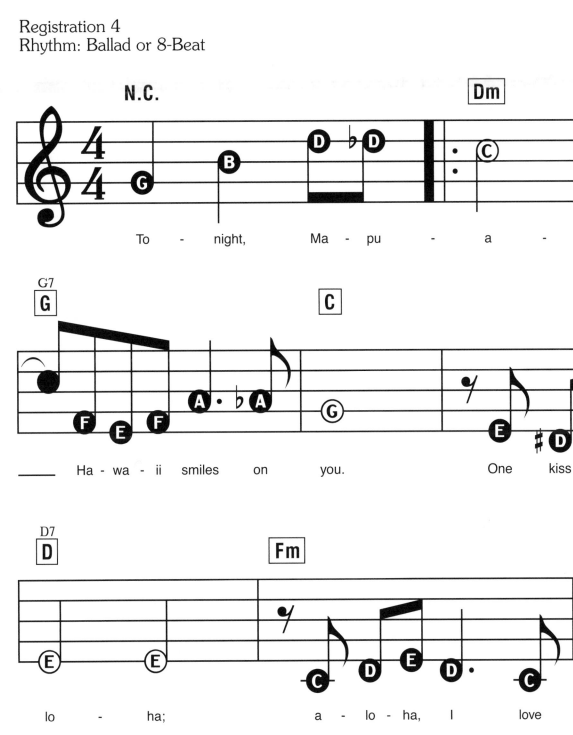

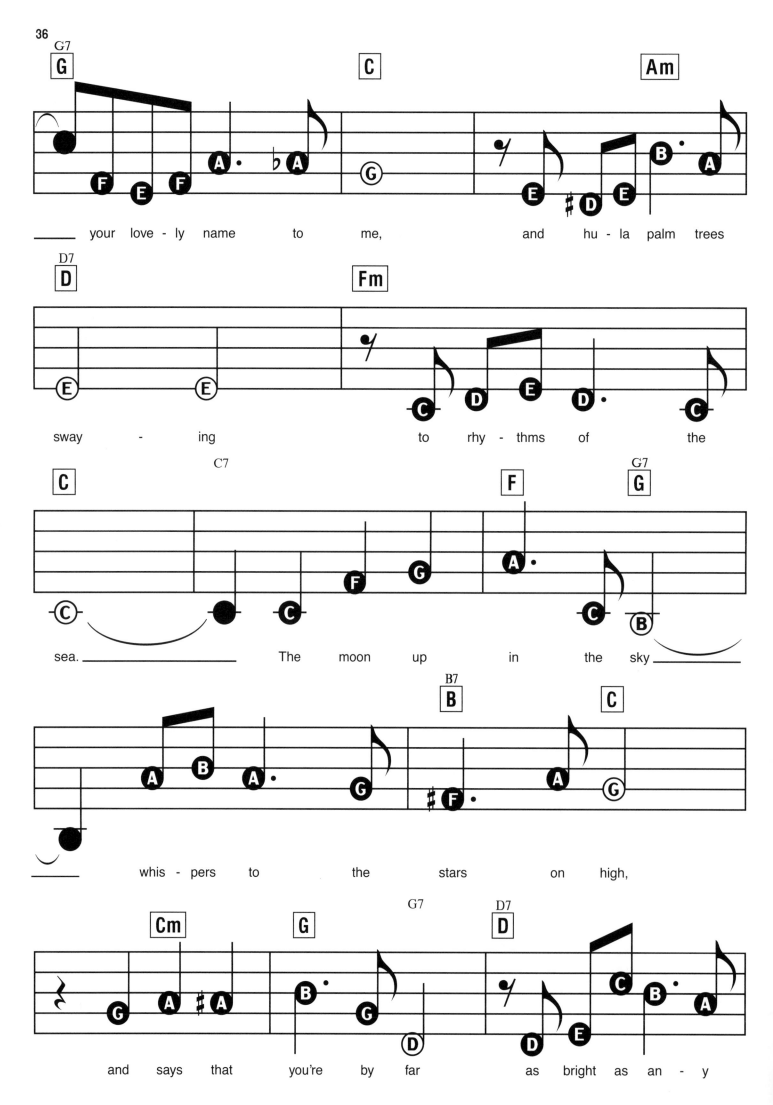

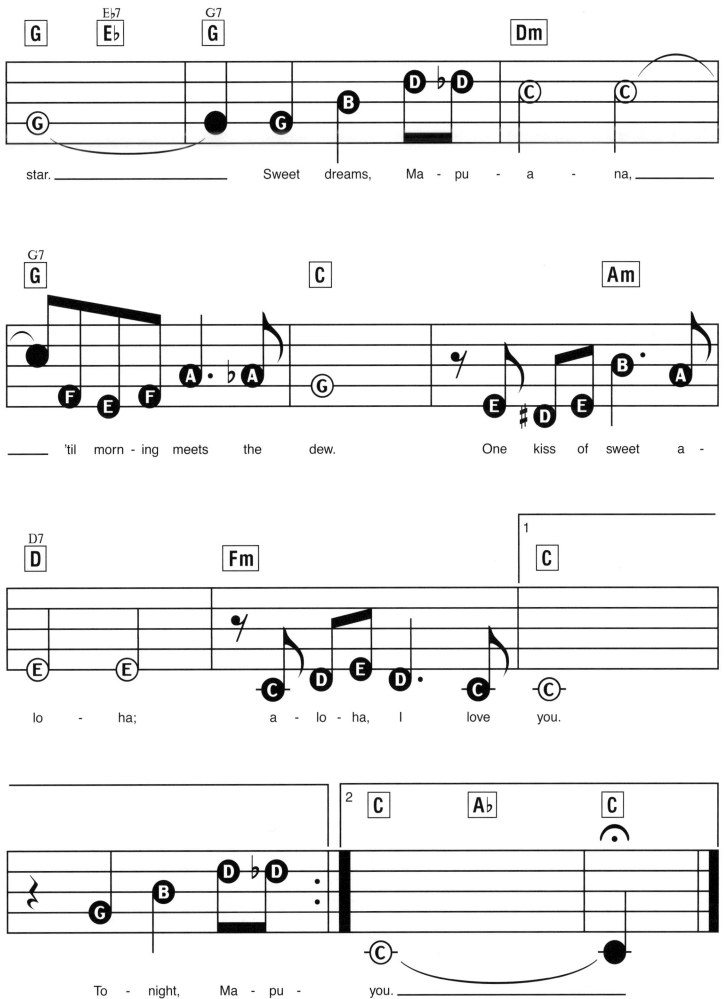

star. _____ Sweet dreams, Ma - pu - a - na, _____

_____ 'til morn - ing meets the dew. One kiss of sweet a -

lo - ha; a - lo - ha, I love you.

To - night, Ma - pu - you. _____

I'll See You in Hawaii

Registration 7
Rhythm: Fox Trot or Ballad

Words and Music by
Tony Todardo

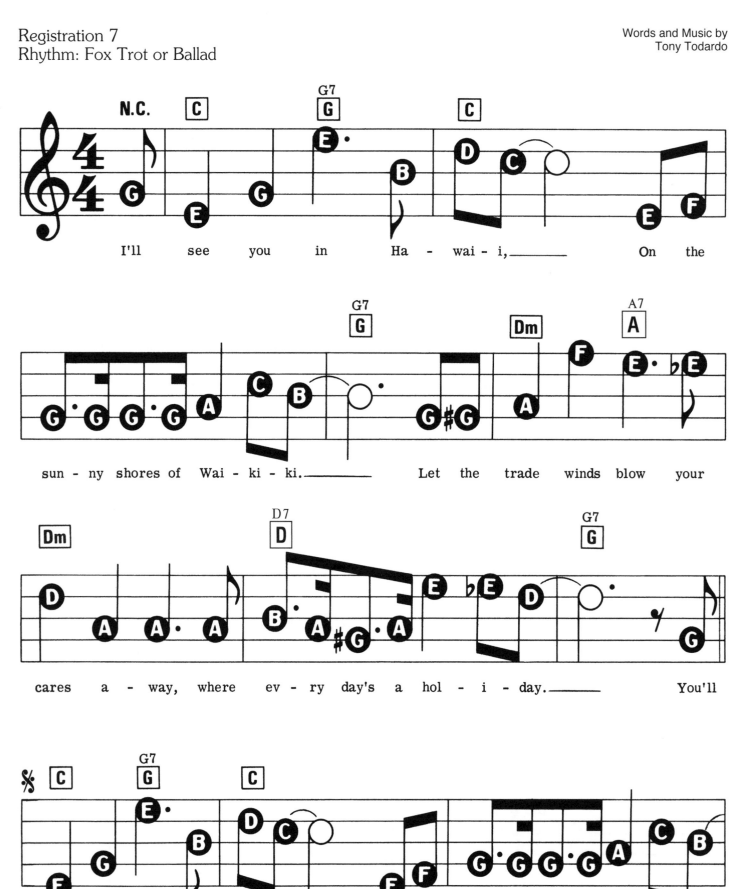

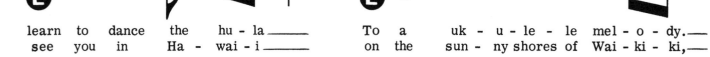

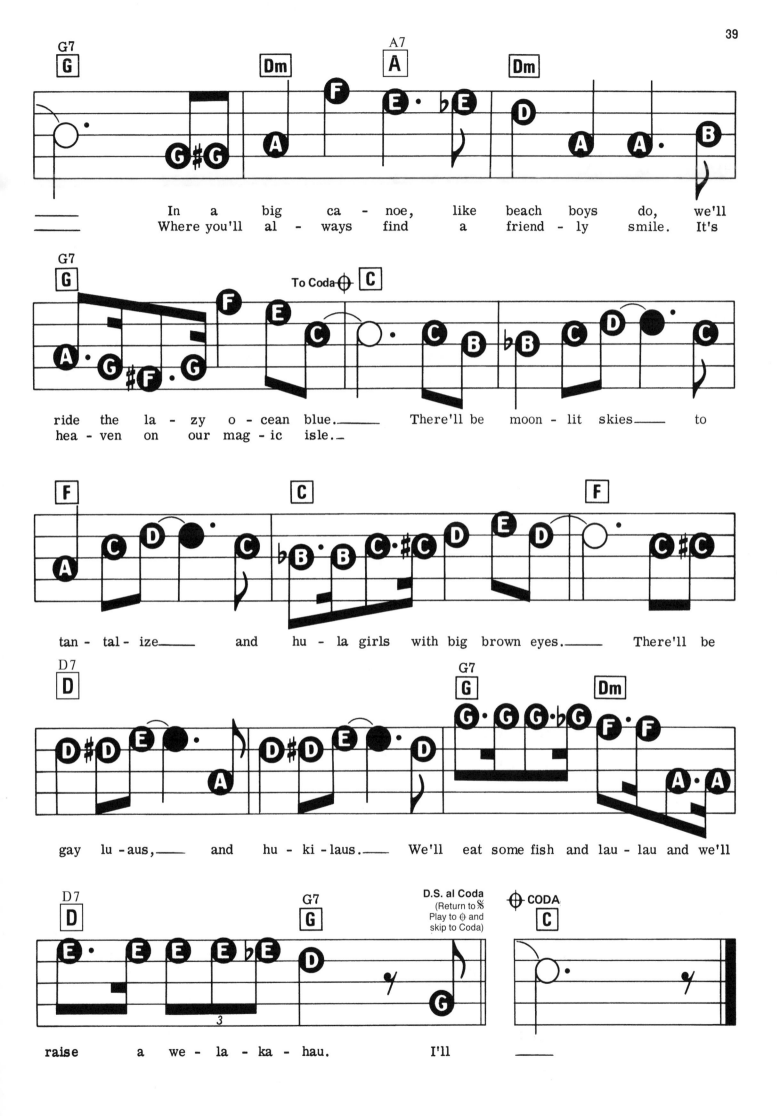

Ka-lu-a

Registration 4
Rhythm: Fox Trot

Words by Anne Caldwell
Music by Jerome Kern

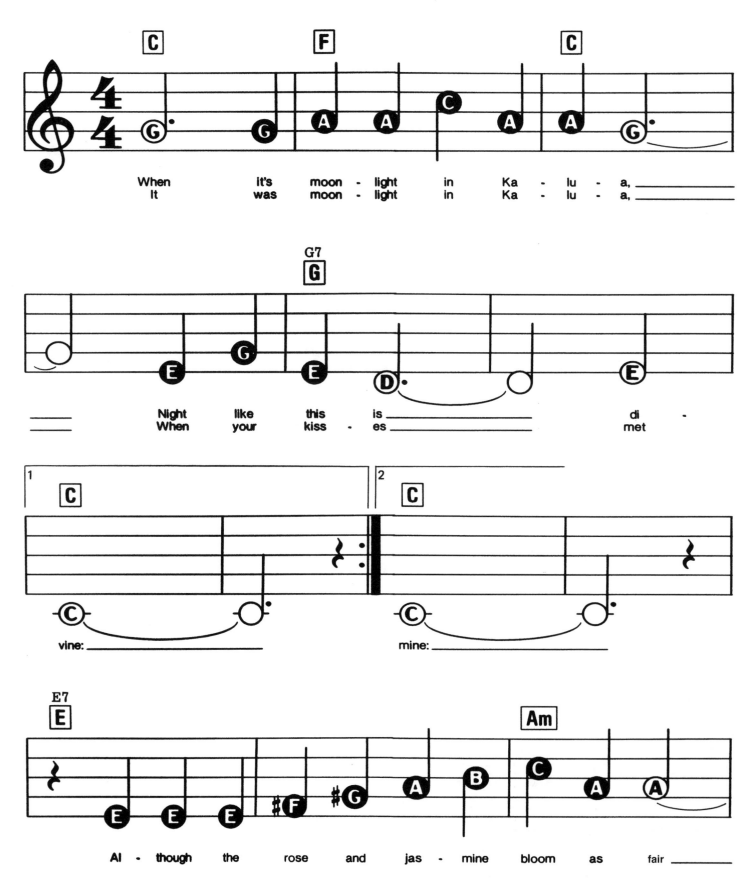

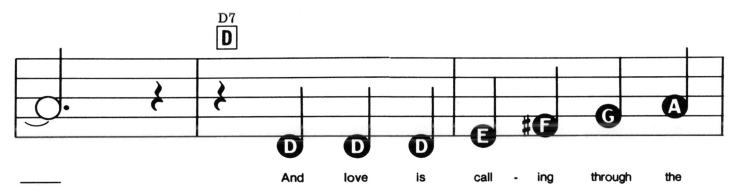

And love is call - ing through the

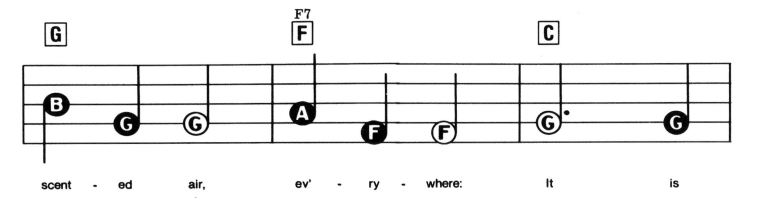

scent - ed air, ev' - ry - where: It is

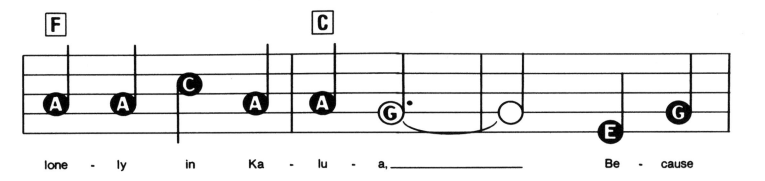

lone - ly in Ka - lu - a,_____ Be - cause

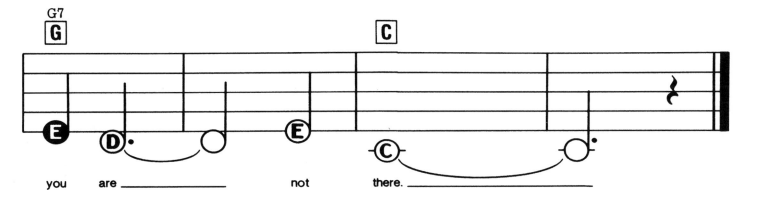

you are _____ not there. _____

(There Goes)
Kealoha

Registration 1
Rhythm: Swing or Ballad

Words by Liko Johnston
Music by Liko Johnston
and Howard Zuenger

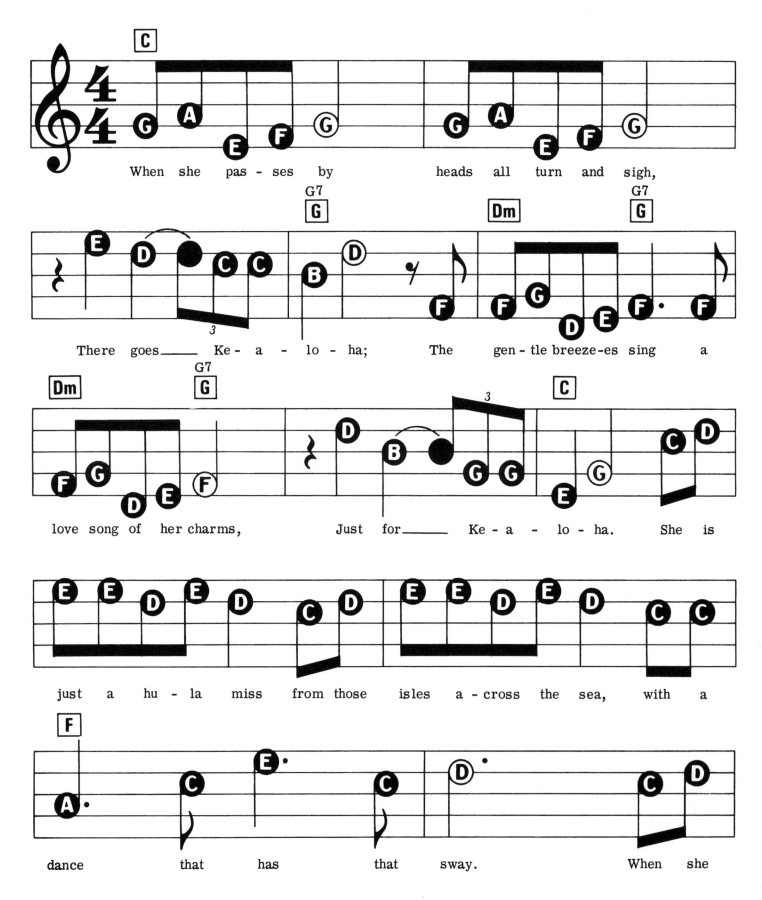

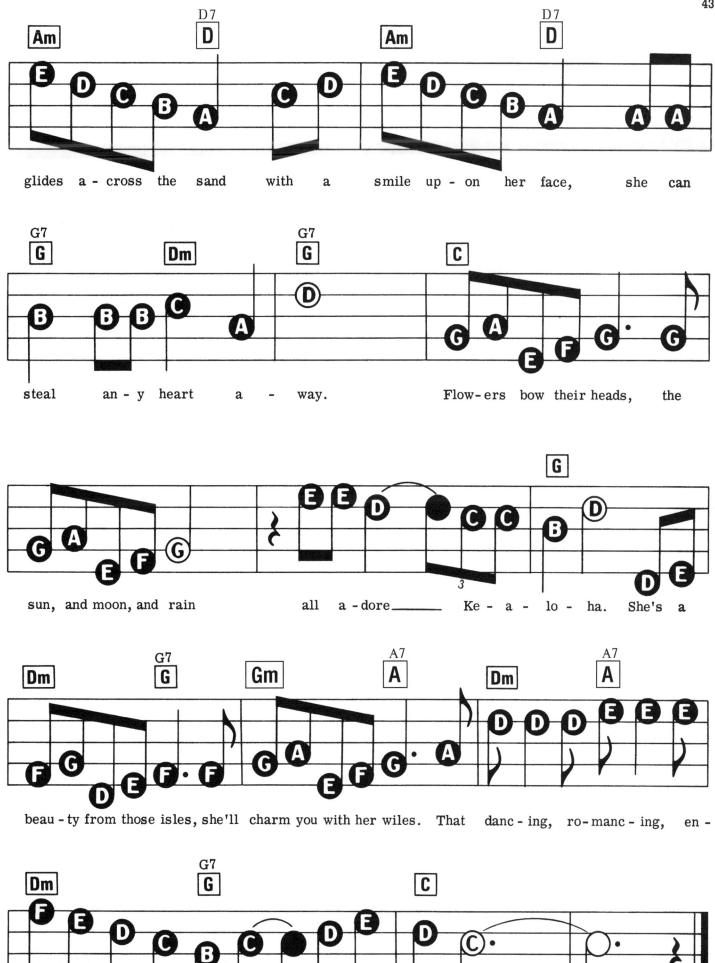

43

Keep Your Eyes on the Hands

Registration 4
Rhythm: Swing

Words and Music by Tony Todaro
and Mary Johnston

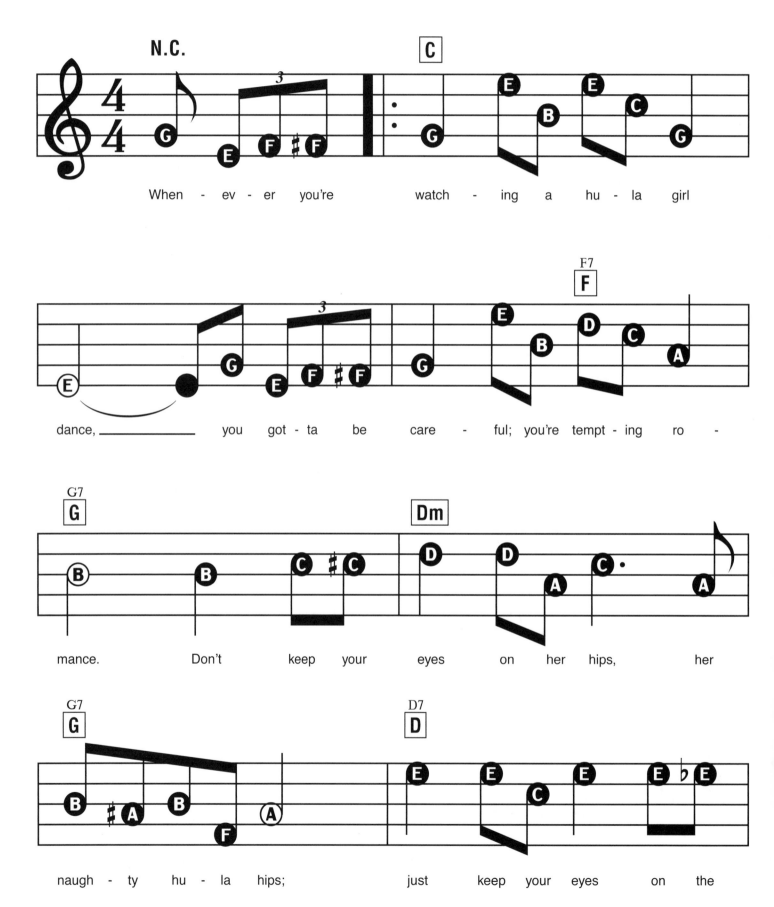

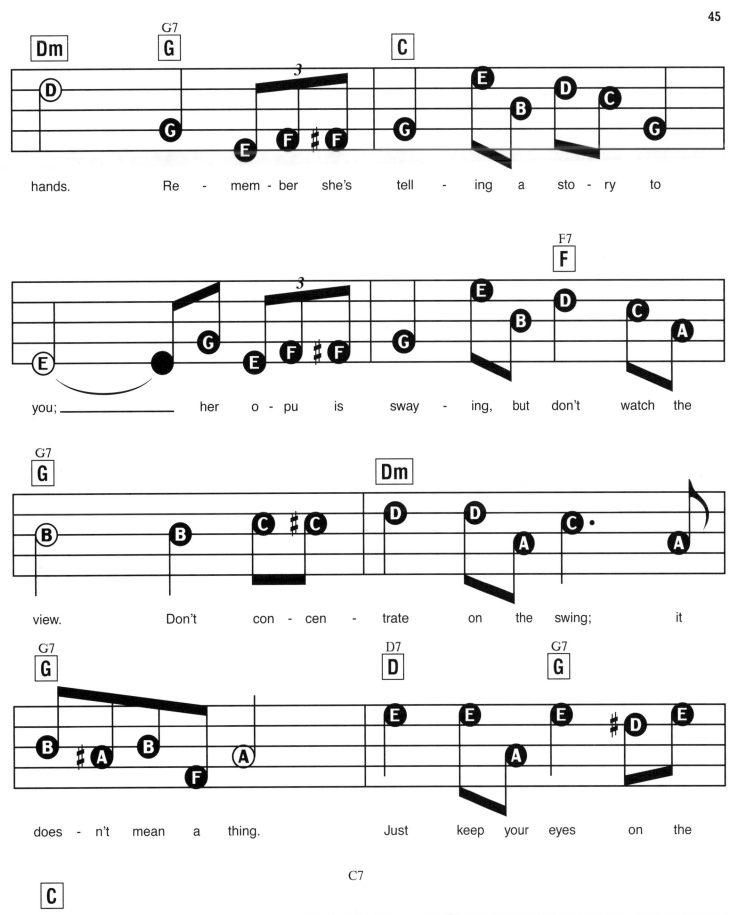

hands.   Re - mem - ber she's tell - ing a sto - ry to

you; _____ her o - pu is sway - ing, but don't watch the

view.   Don't con - cen - trate on the swing;   it

does - n't mean a thing.   Just keep your eyes on the

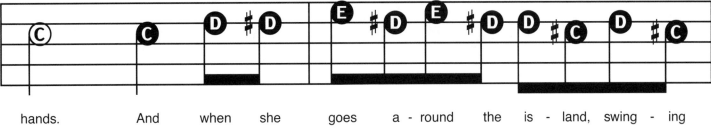

hands.   And when she goes a - round the is - land, swing - ing

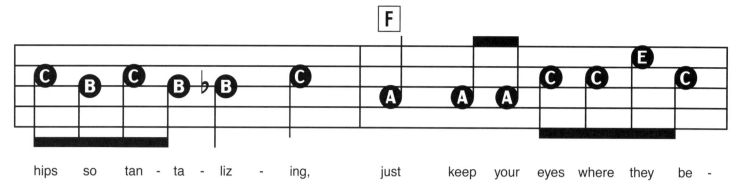

hips so tan - ta - liz - ing, just keep your eyes where they be -

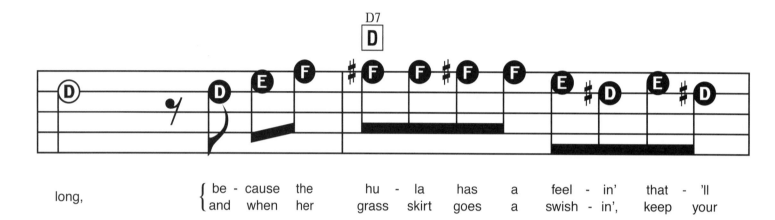

long,　　{ be - cause the hu - la has a feel - in' that - 'll
　　　　{ and when her grass skirt goes a swish - in', keep your

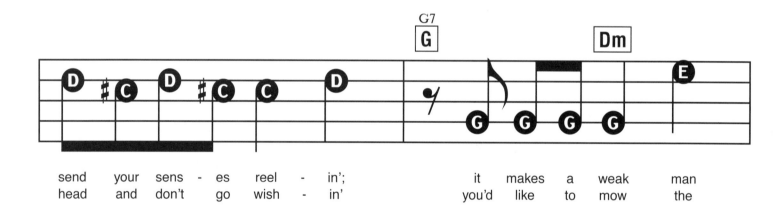

send your sens - es reel - in'; it makes a weak man
head and don't go wish - in' you'd like to mow the

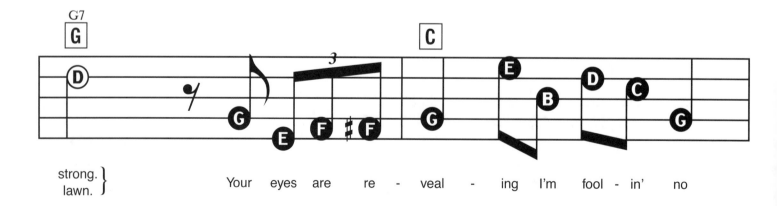

strong. } Your eyes are re - veal - ing I'm fool - in' no
lawn. }

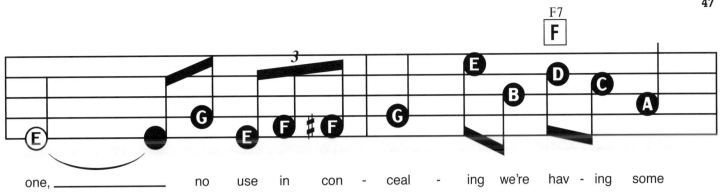

one, _____ no use in con - ceal - ing we're hav - ing some

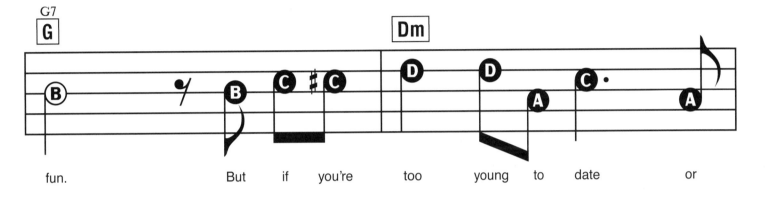

fun. But if you're too young to date or

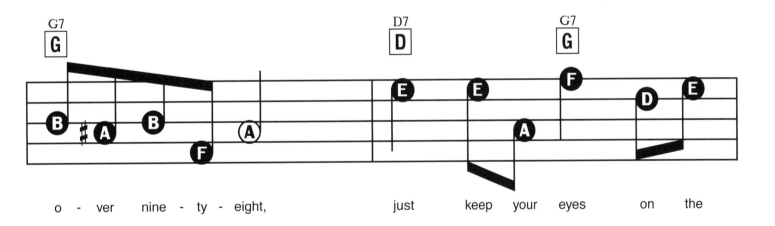

o - ver nine - ty - eight, just keep your eyes on the

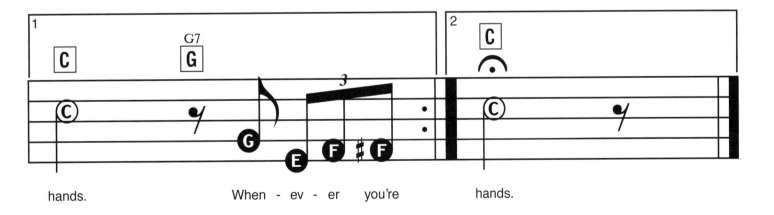

hands. When - ev - er you're hands.

Ku-u-i-po
(Hawaiian Sweetheart)
from SLIVER

Registration 4
Rhythm: Swing

Words and Music by Luigi Creatore,
George Weiss and Hugo Peretti

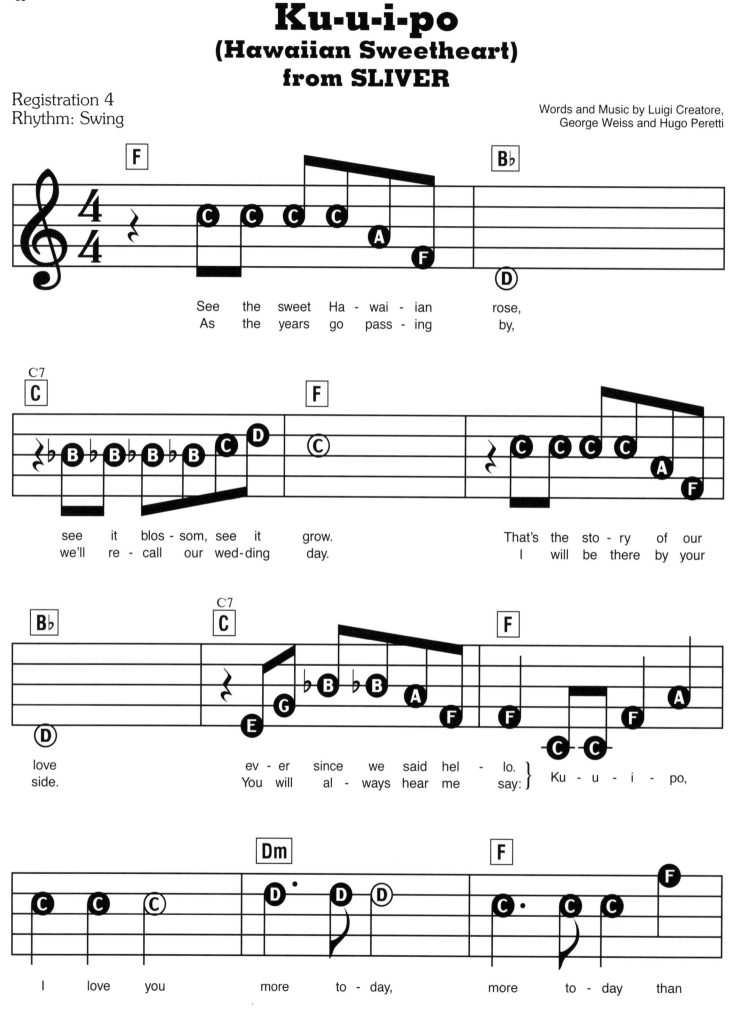

See the sweet Ha - wai - ian rose,
As the years go pass - ing by,

see it blos - som, see it grow.
we'll re - call our wed - ding day.

That's the sto - ry of our
I will be there by your

love
side.

ev - er since we said hel - lo.
You will al - ways hear me say:

Ku - u - i - po,

I love you more to - day, more to - day than

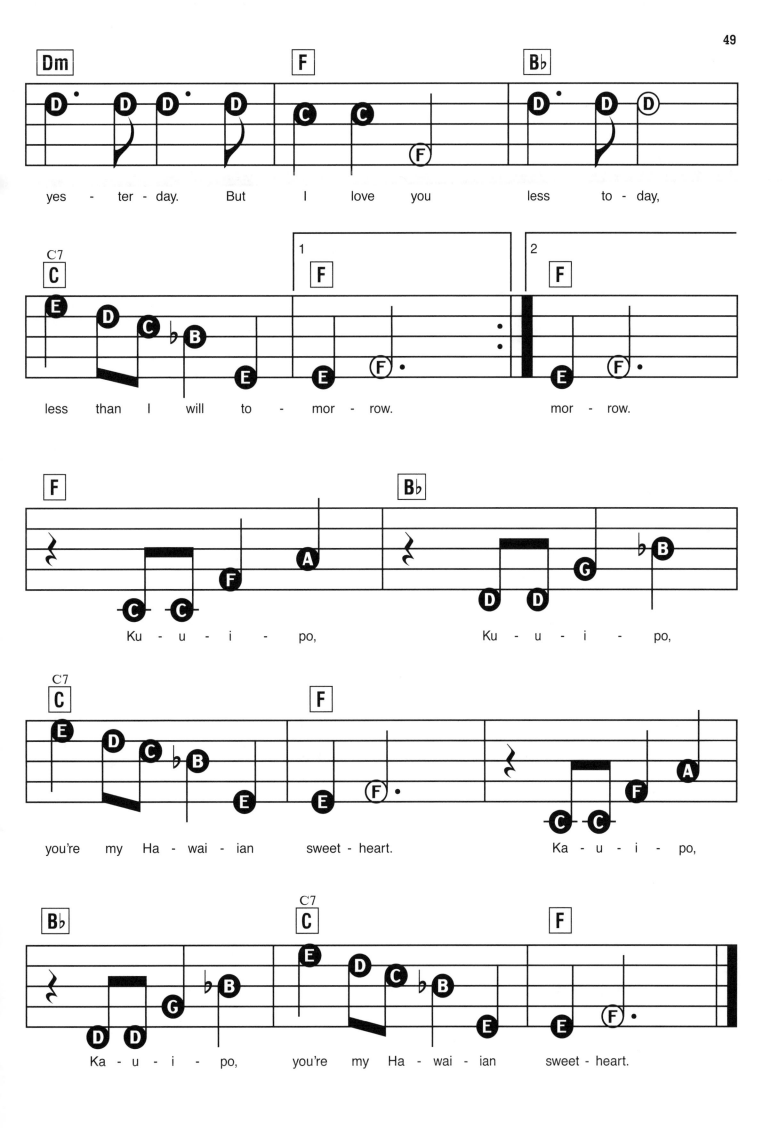

Lovely Hula Girl

Registration 1
Rhythm: Fox Trot or Ballad

Words and Music by Jack Pitman
and Randy Oness

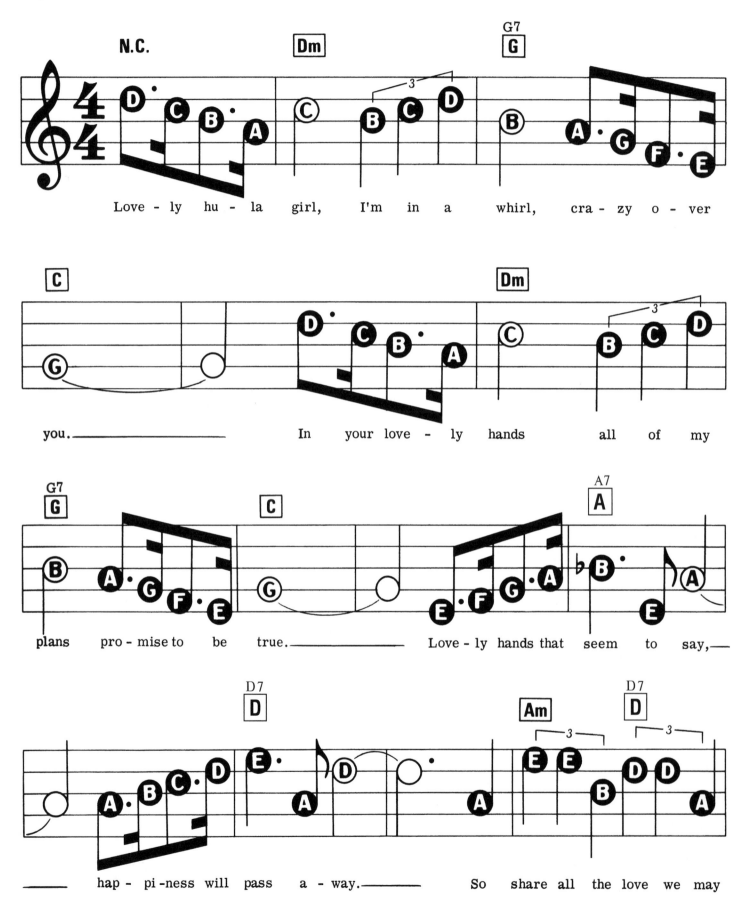

Love - ly hu - la girl, I'm in a whirl, cra - zy o - ver

you._____ In your love - ly hands all of my

plans pro - mise to be true._____ Love - ly hands that seem to say,_____

_____ hap - pi -ness will pass a - way._____ So share all the love we may

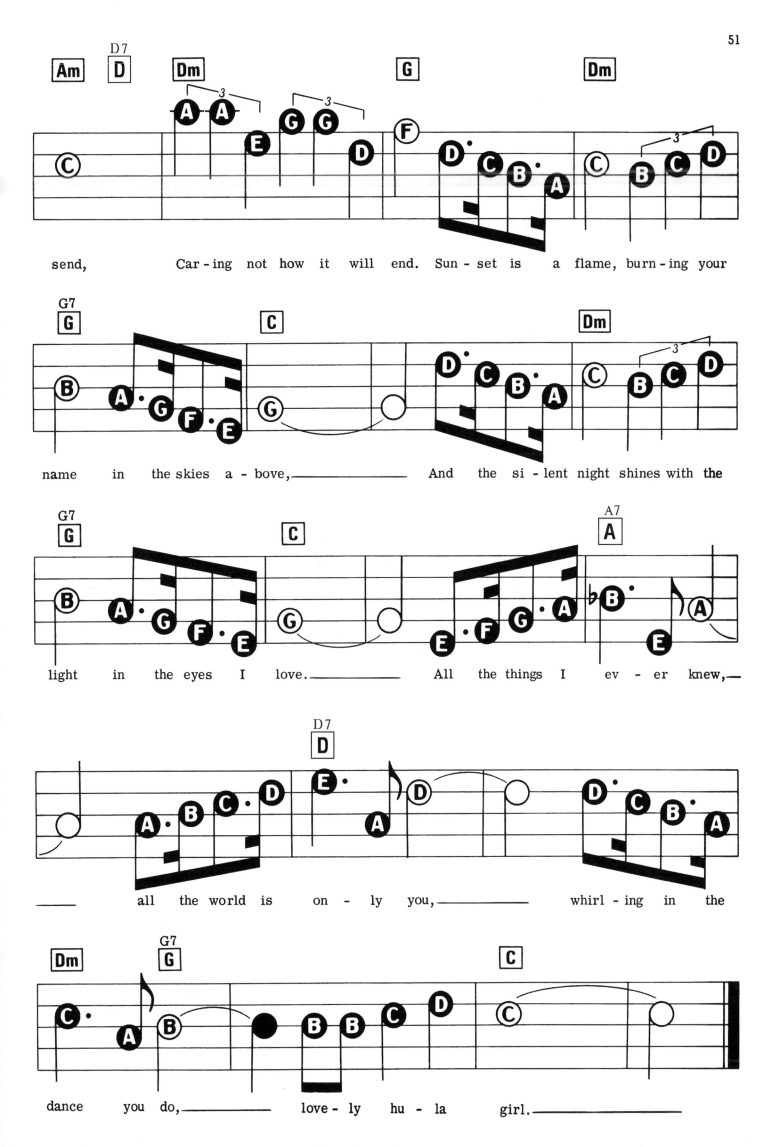

Lovely Hula Hands

Registration 3
Rhythm: Fox Trot or Swing

Words and Music by
R. Alex Anderson

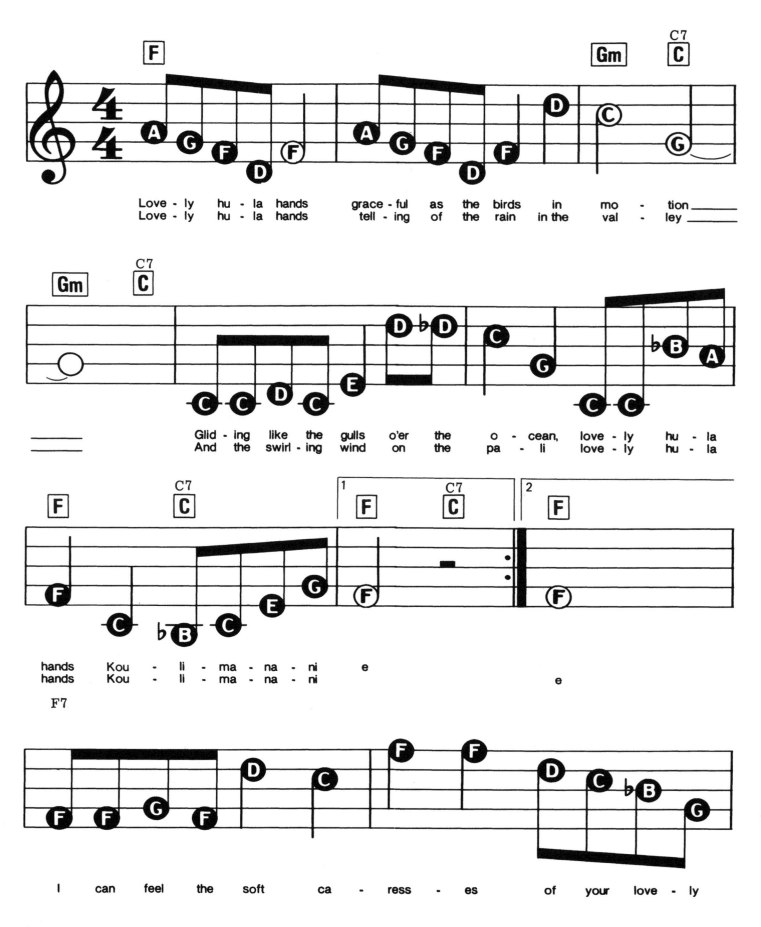

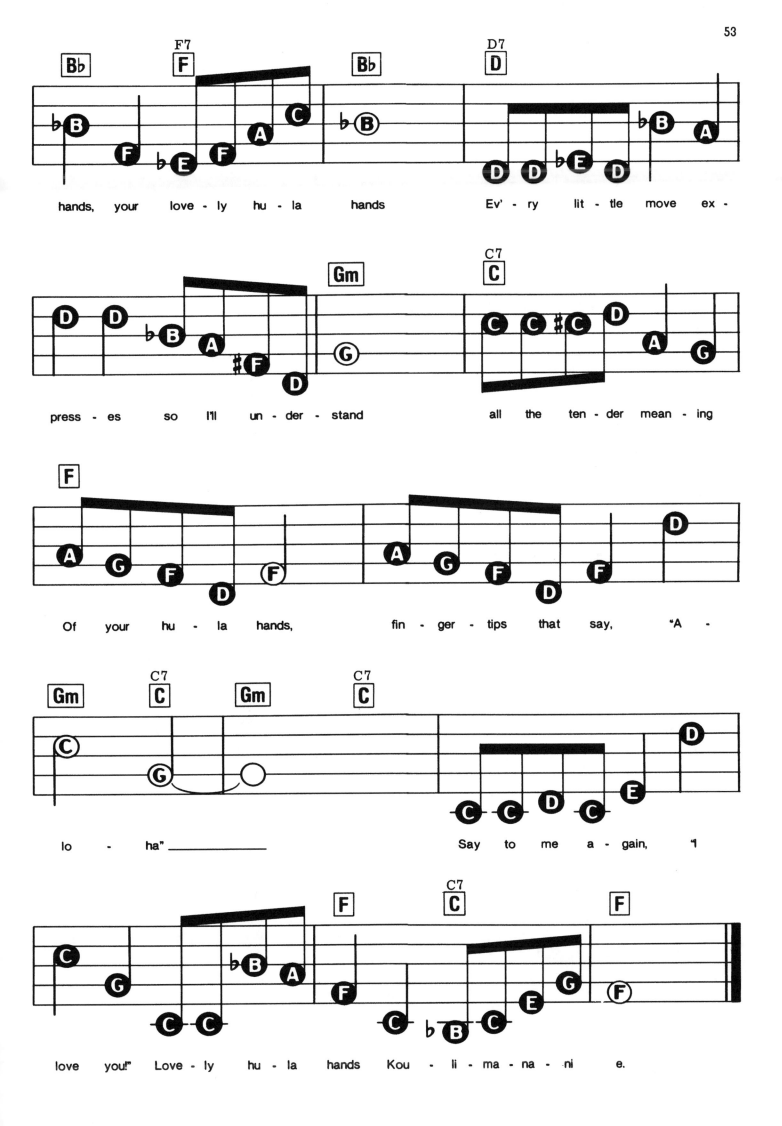

53

Maui Waltz

Registration 3
Rhythm: Waltz

Words and Music by
Bob Nelson

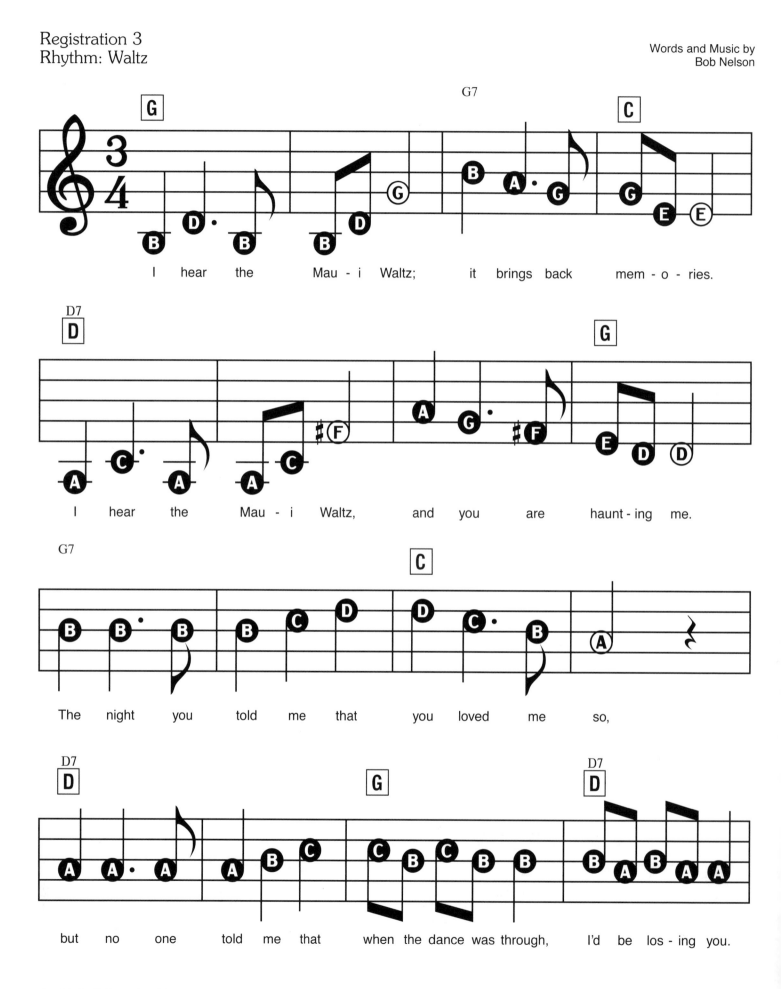

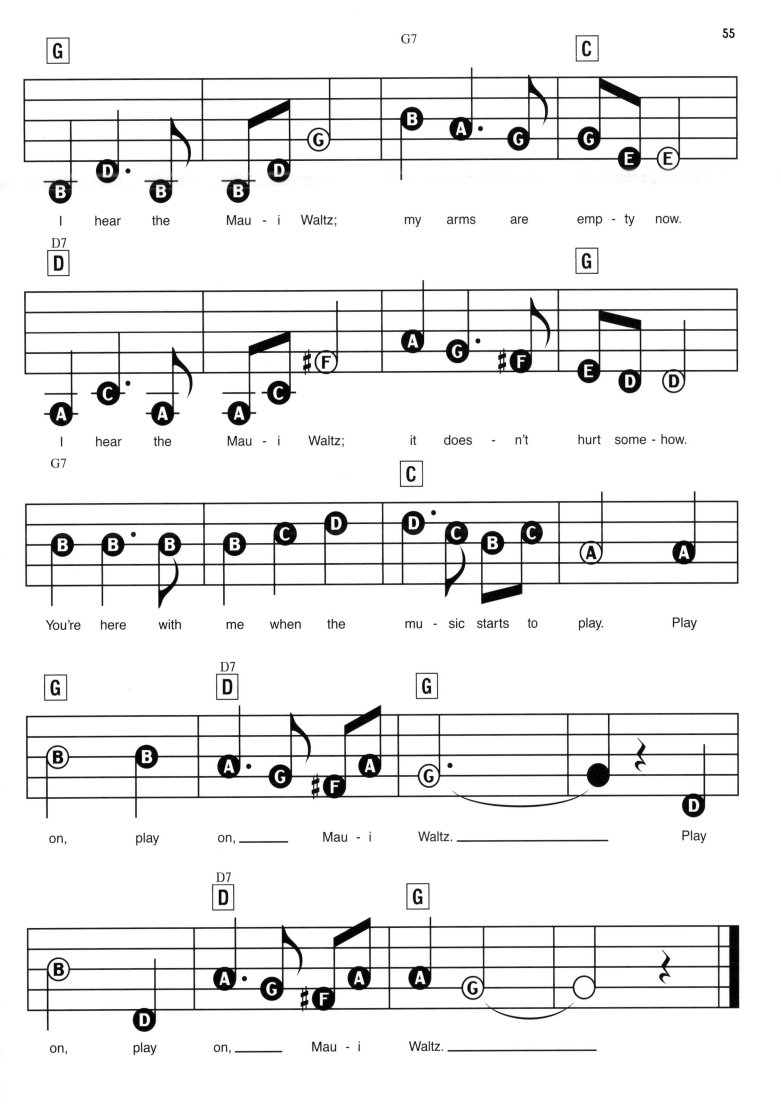

Mele Kalikimaka

Registration 5
Rhythm: Fox Trot or Swing

Words and Music by
R. Alex Anderson

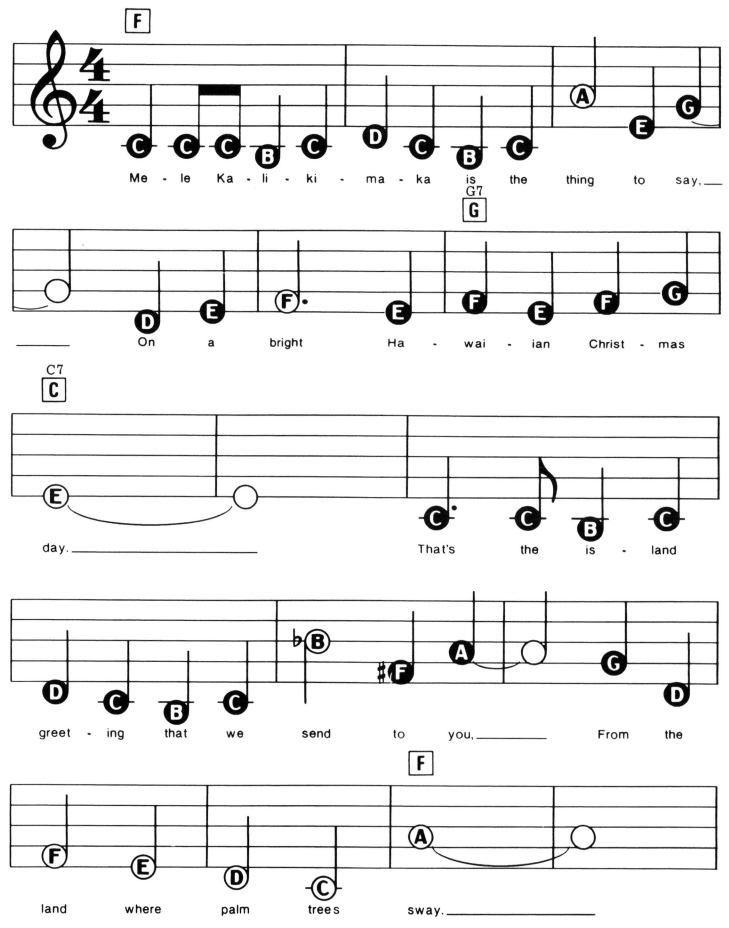

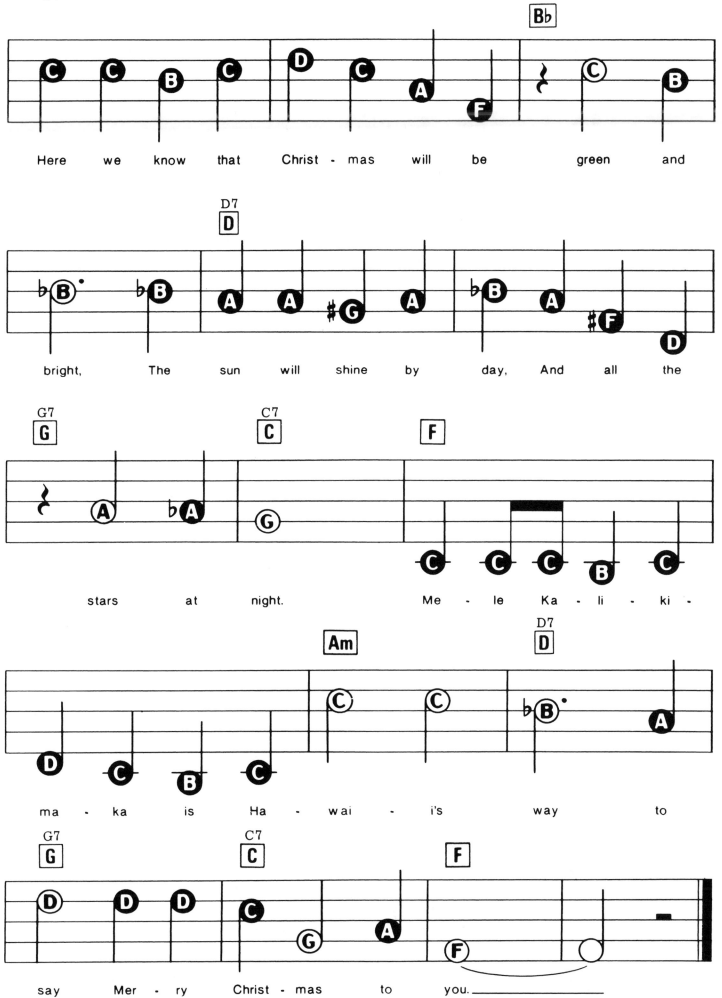

My Little Grass Shack
in Kealakekua, Hawaii

Registration 4
Rhythm: Swing

Words and Music by Bill Cogswell,
Tommy Harrison and Johnny Noble

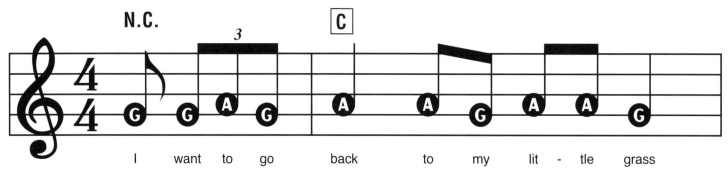

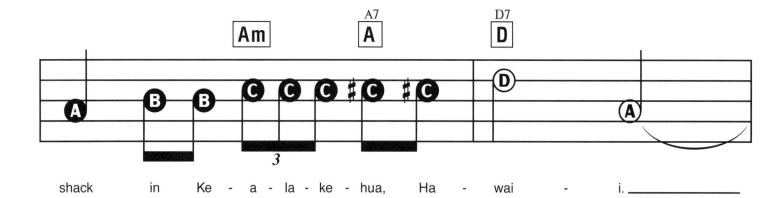

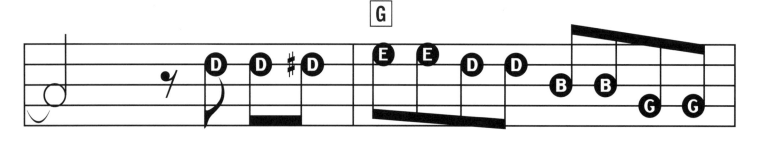

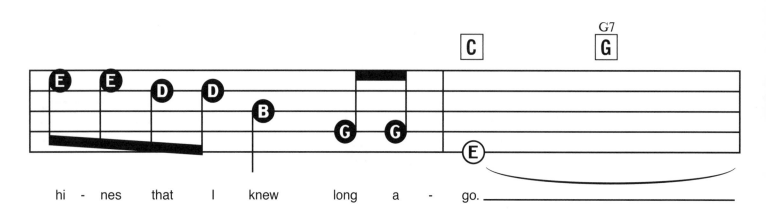

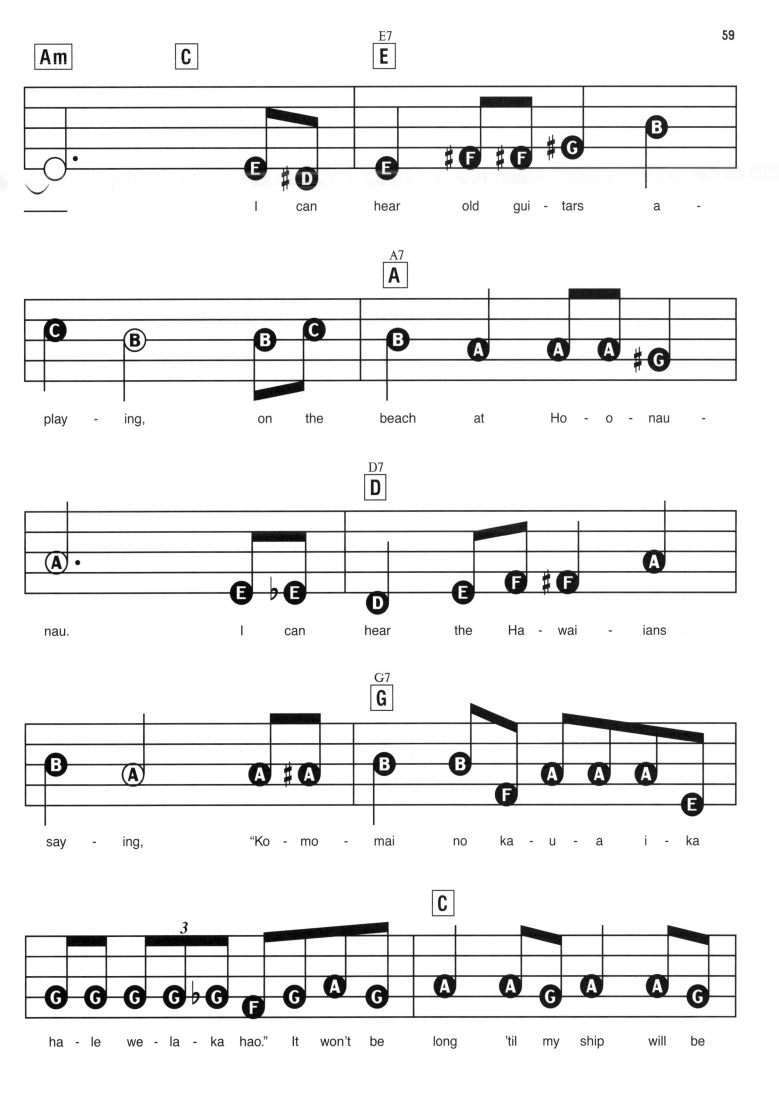

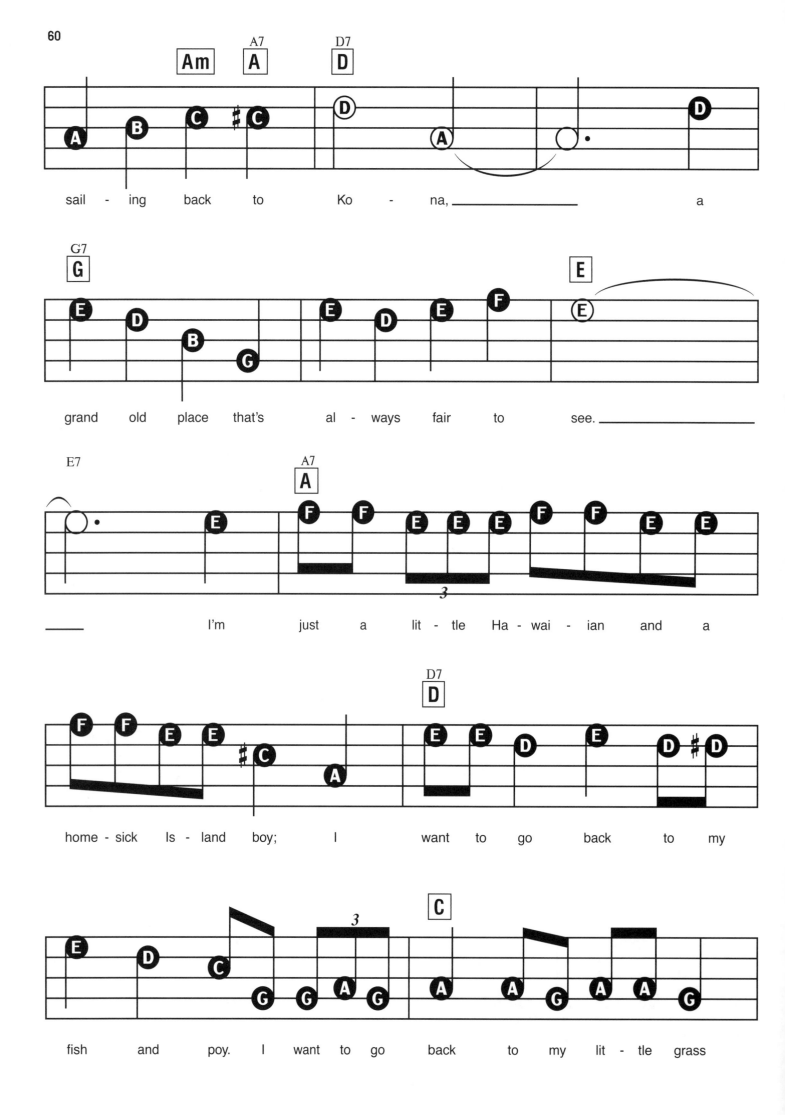

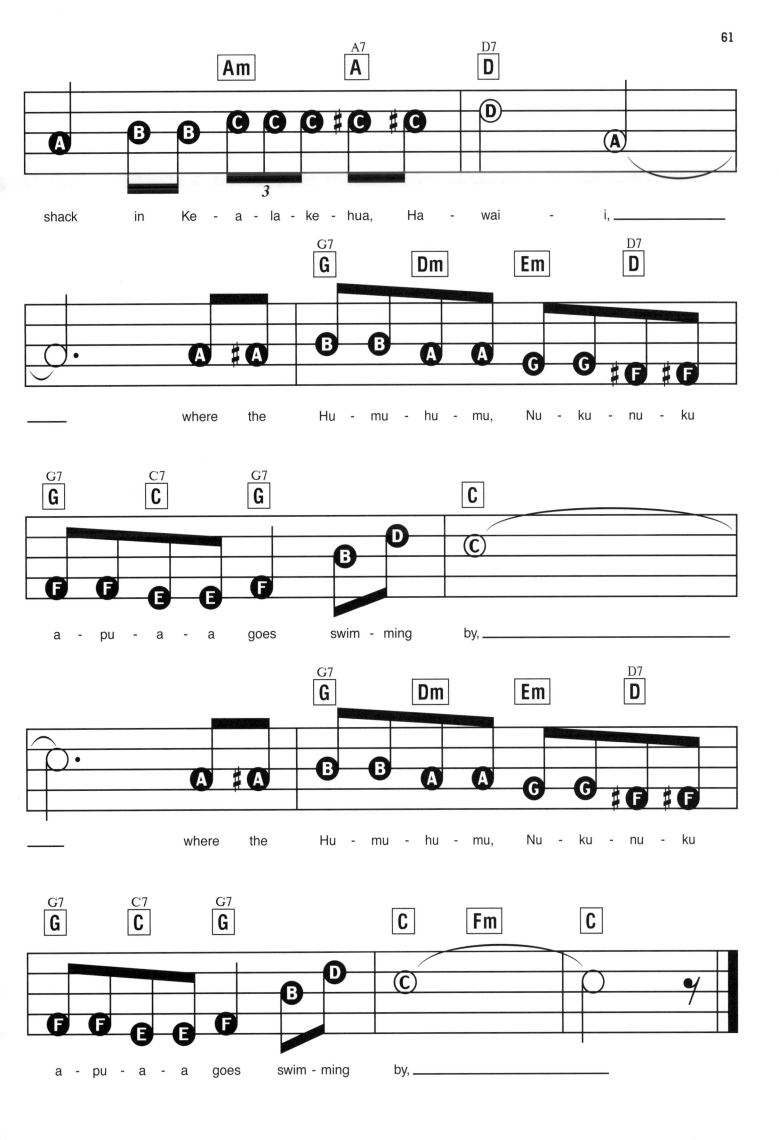

Now Is the Hour
(Maori Farewell Song)

Registration 9
Rhythm: Waltz

Words and Music by Clement Scott,
Maewa Kaithau and Dorothy Stewart

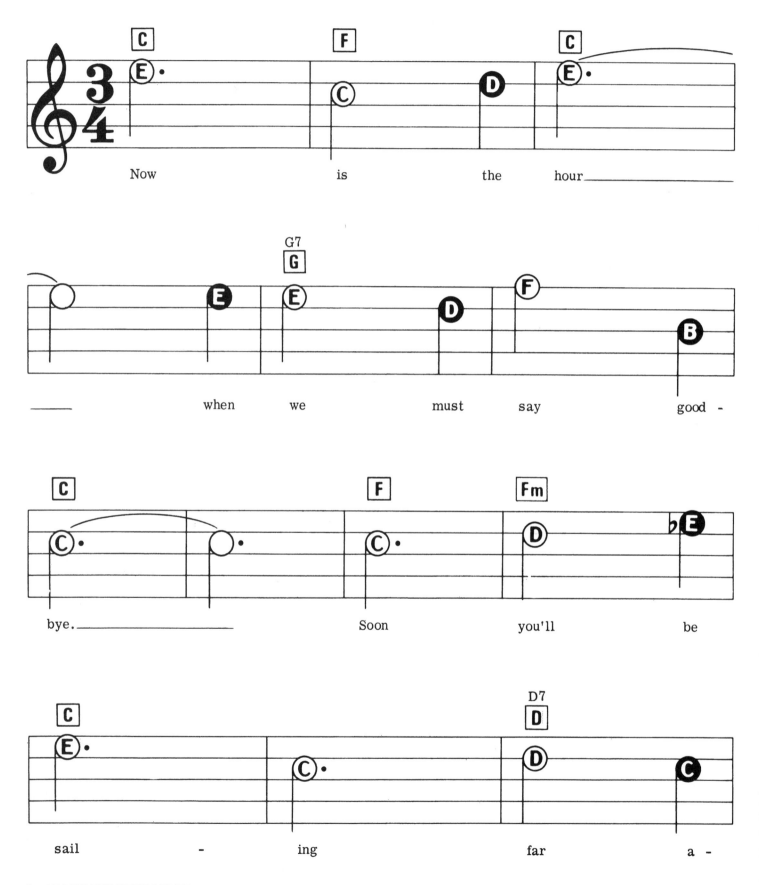

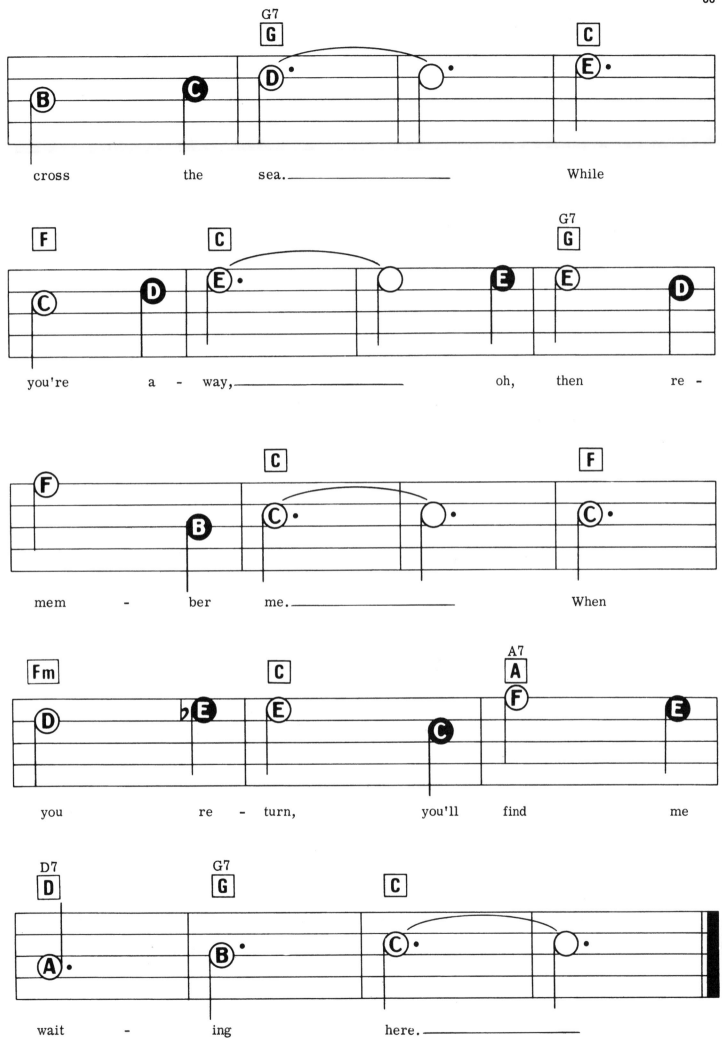

63

On the Beach at Waikiki

Registration 4
Rhythm: Fox Trot or Swing

Words by G.H. Stover
Music by Henry Kailimaie

Over the Rainbow
from THE WIZARD OF OZ

Registration 5
Rhythm: Ballad

Music by Harold Arlen
Lyric by E.Y. "Yip" Harburg

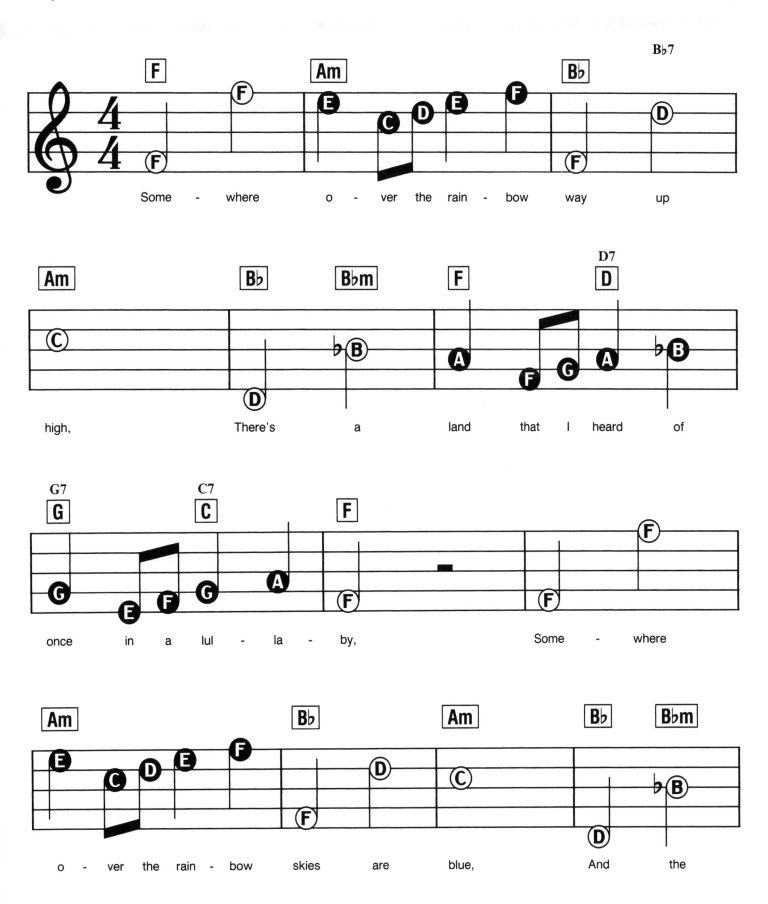

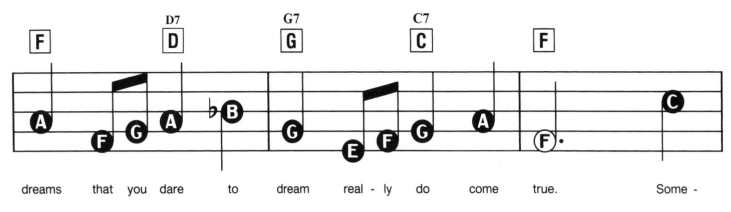

dreams that you dare to dream real - ly do come true. Some -

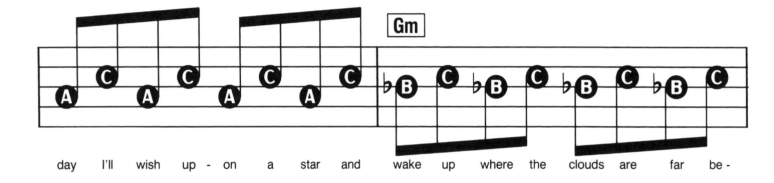

day I'll wish up - on a star and wake up where the clouds are far be -

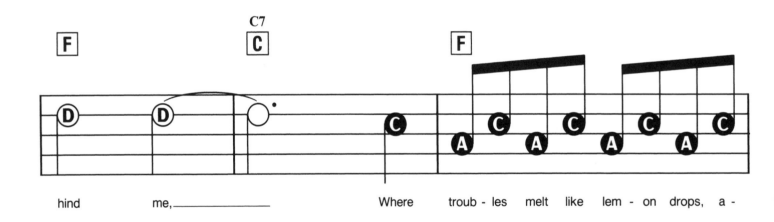

hind me,_____ Where troub - les melt like lem - on drops, a -

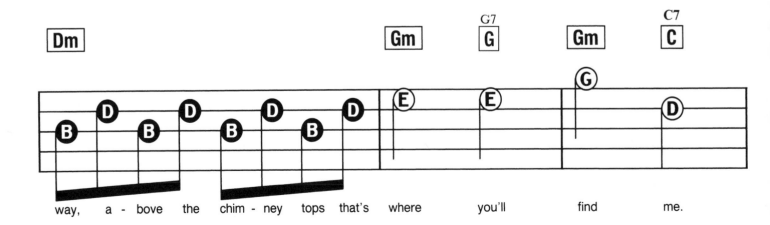

way, a - bove the chim - ney tops that's where you'll find me.

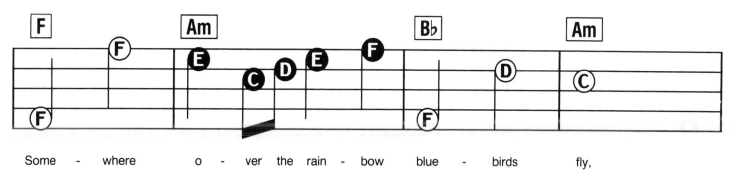

Some - where o - ver the rain - bow blue - birds fly,

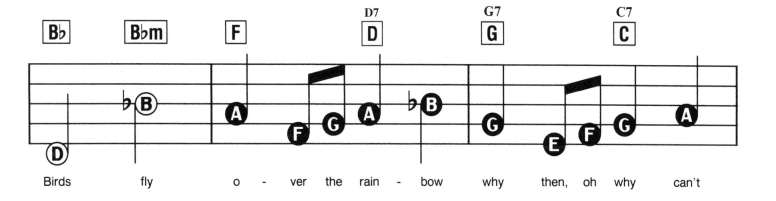

Birds fly o - ver the rain - bow why then, oh why can't

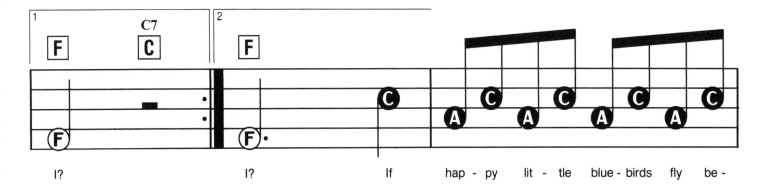

I? I? If hap - py lit - tle blue - birds fly be -

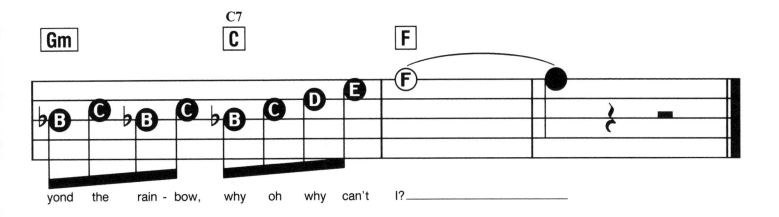

yond the rain - bow, why oh why can't I?

One Paddle, Two Paddle

Registration 7
Rhythm: Swing or Jazz

Words and Music by
Kui Lee

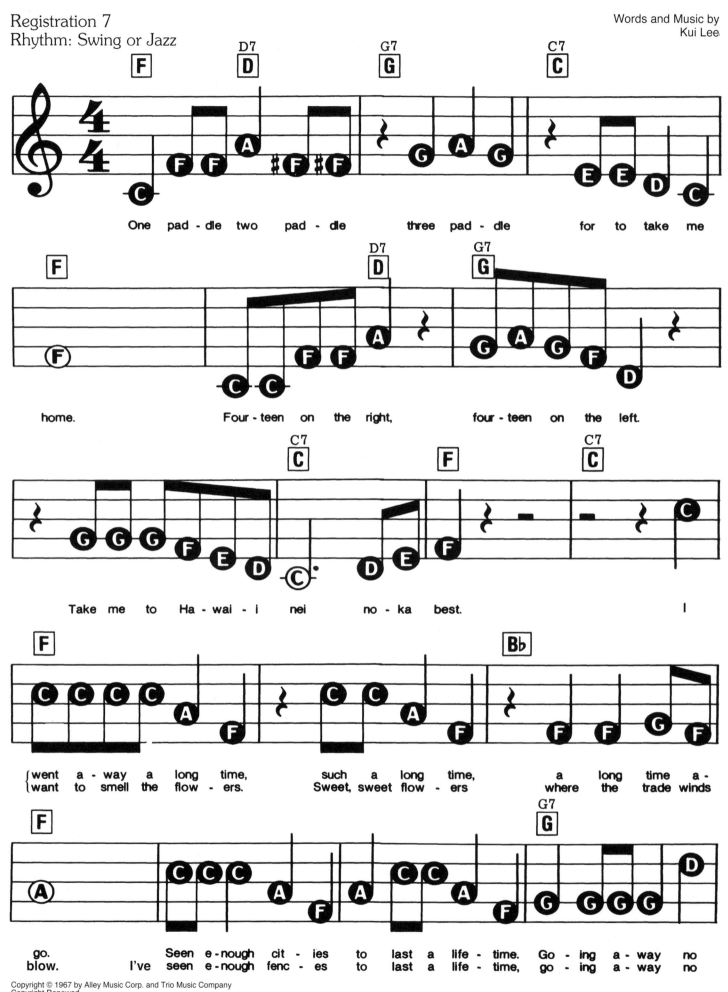

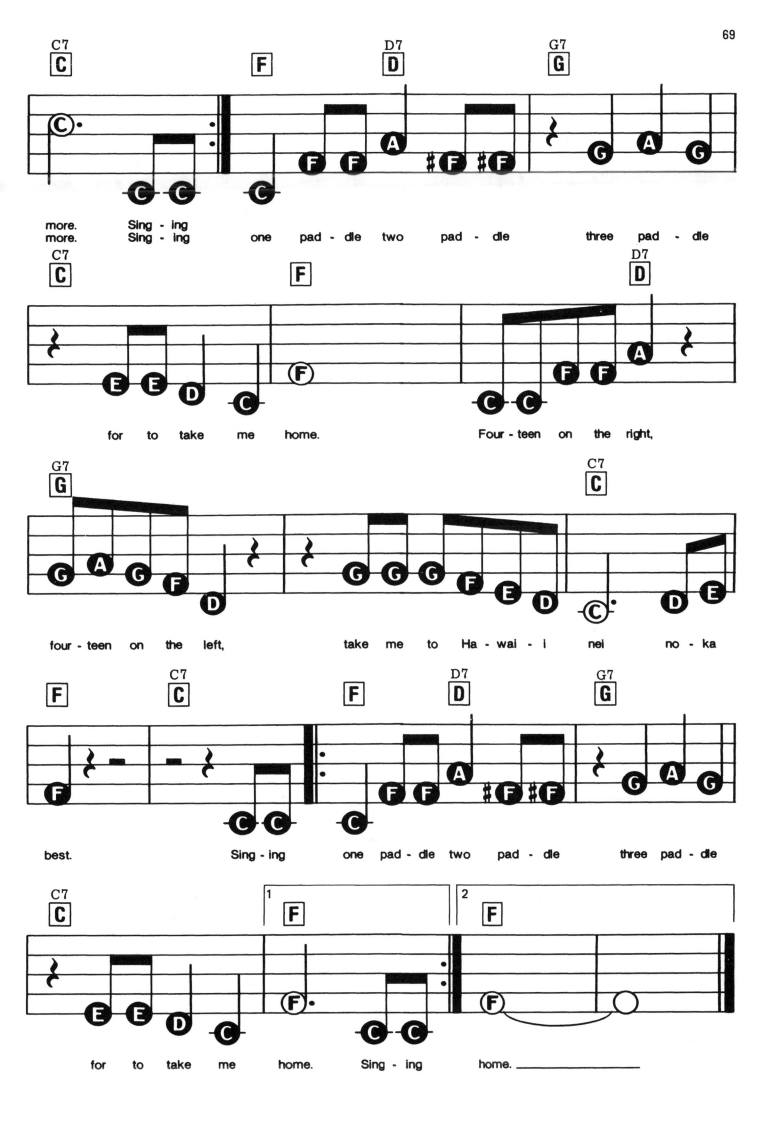

Our Love and Aloha

Registration 3
Rhythm: Ballad or Swing

Words and Music by
Leolani Blaisdell

When the Lur - line_____ sails a - way, Smile your

sweet_____ and win - some way_____ and take with you our_____

love and a - lo - ha_____ With a to - ken_____ flow - er

lei and a kiss_____ for you this day,_____ we give to

you our_____ love and a - lo - ha._____

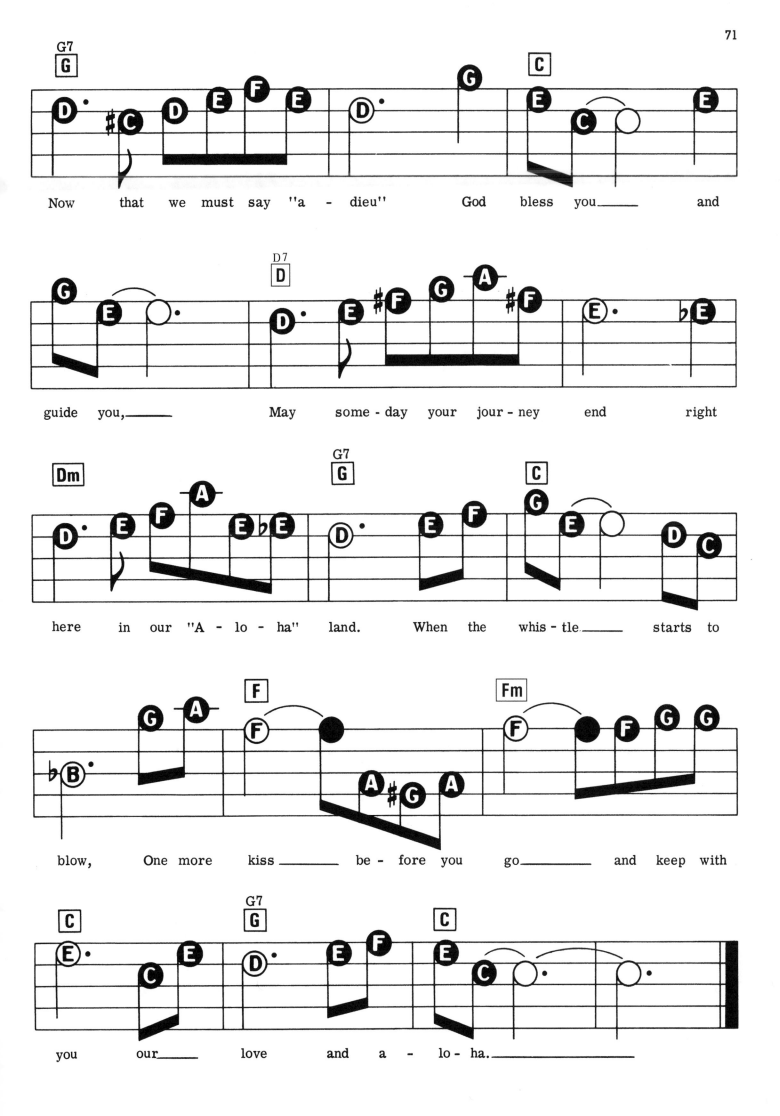

Pagan Love Song

Registration 4
Rhythm: Waltz

Words and Music by Nacio Herb Brown
and Arthur Freed

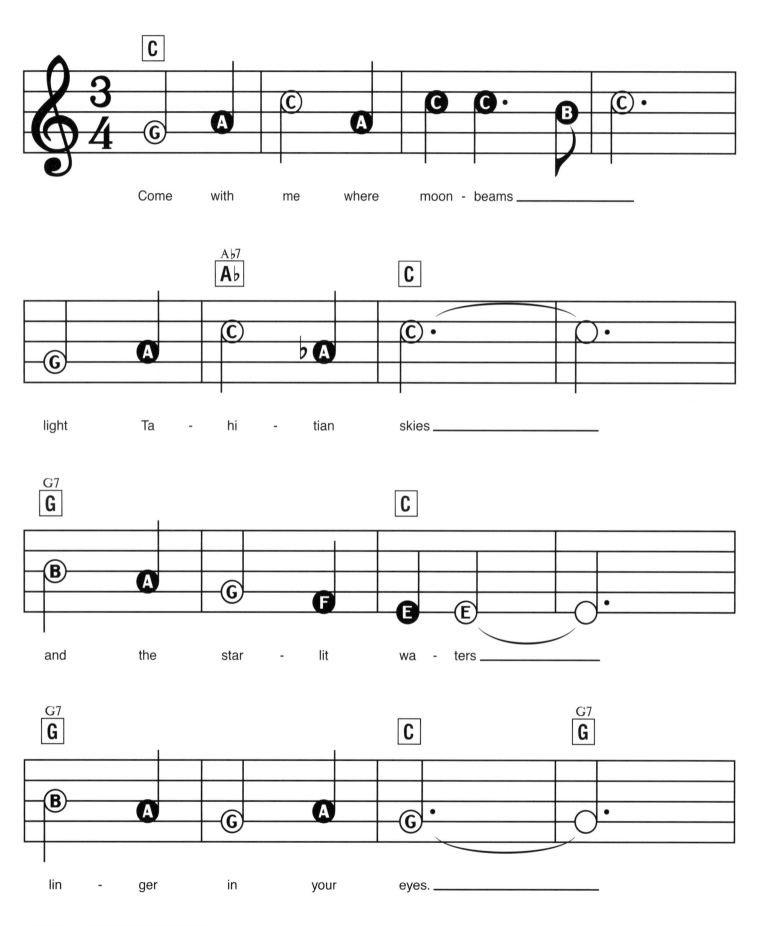

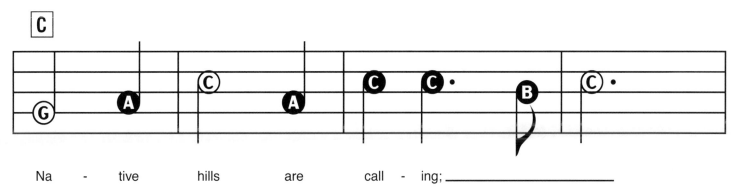

Na - tive hills are call - ing; _____

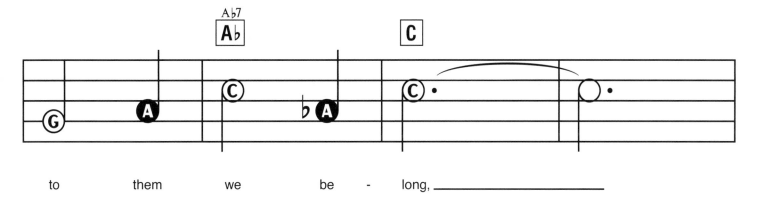

to them we be - long, _____

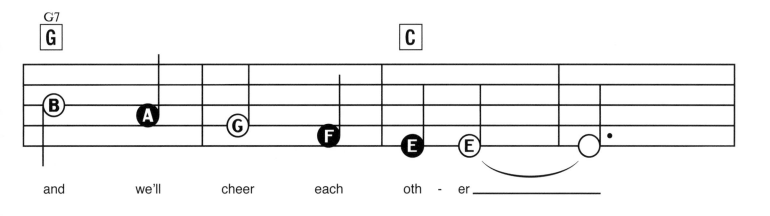

and we'll cheer each oth - er _____

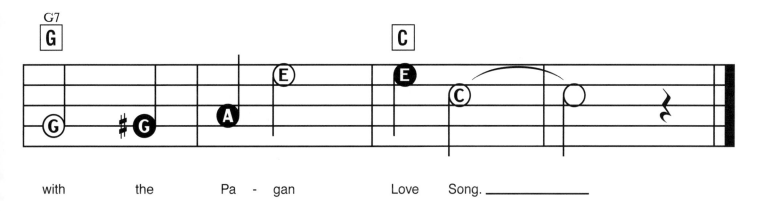

with the Pa - gan Love Song. _____

Pearly Shells
(Pupu O Ewa)

Registration 5
Rhythm: Swing

Words and Music by Webley Edwards
and Leon Pober

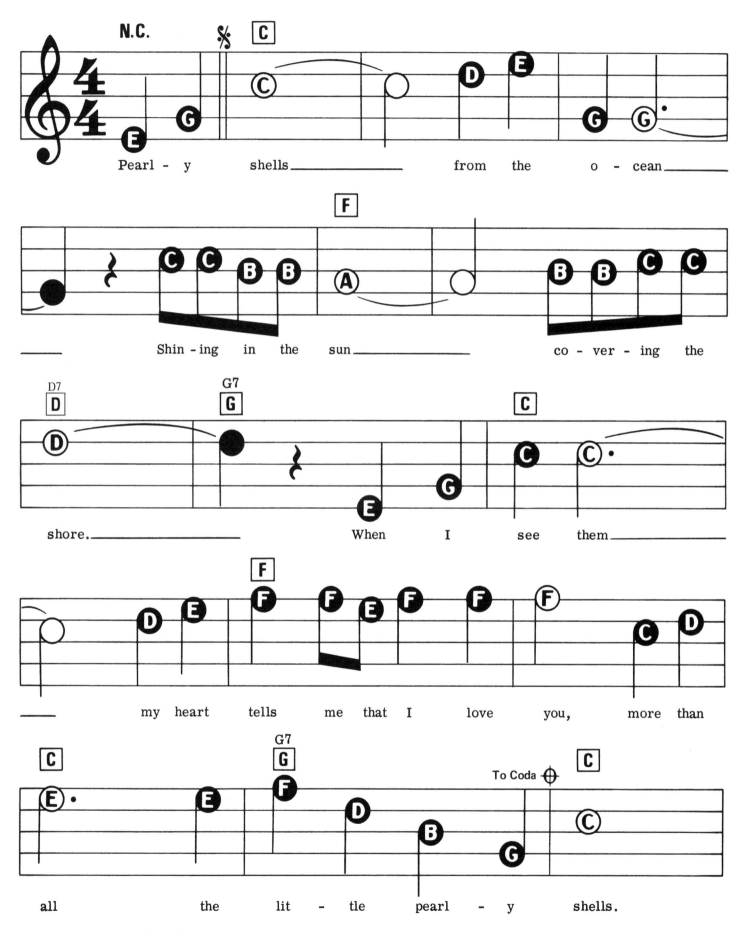

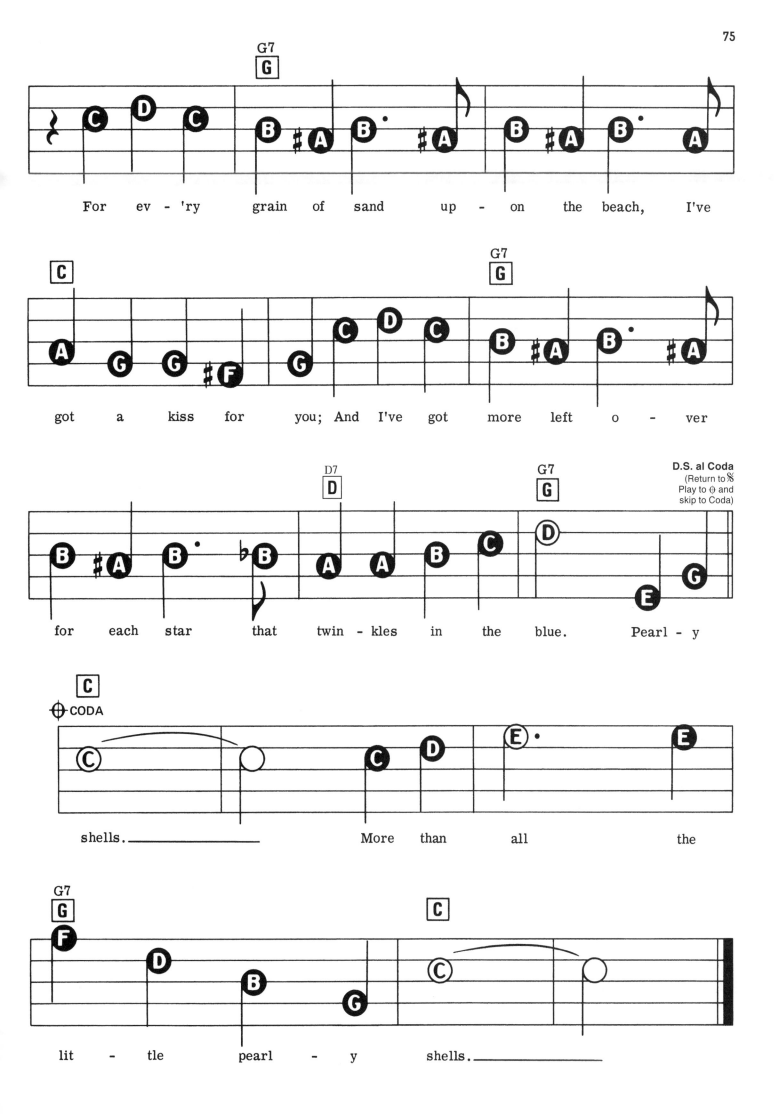

Sands of Waikiki

Registration 4
Rhythm: Ballad or Slow Rock

Words and Music by
Jack Pitman

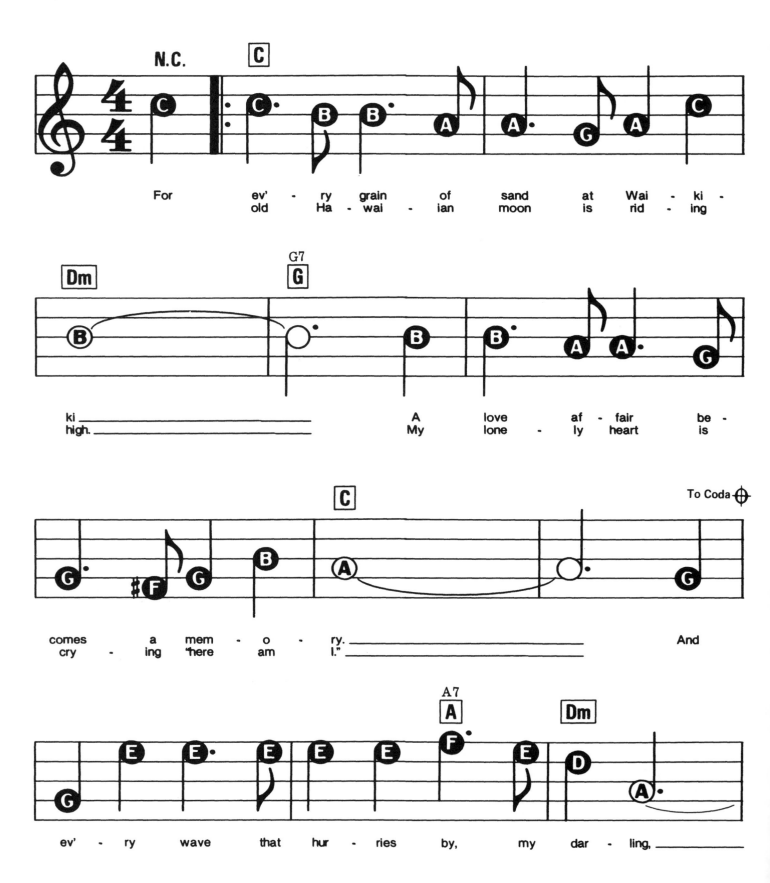

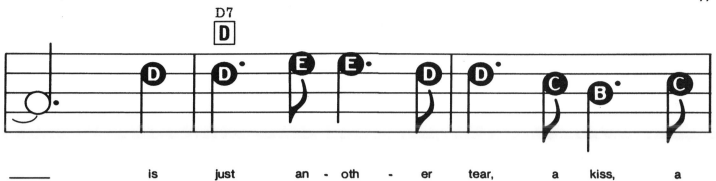

is just an - oth - er tear, a kiss, a

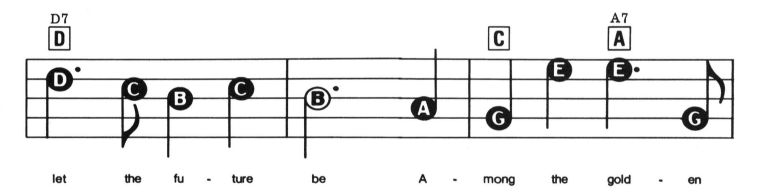

sigh. _____ The Take me, make me yours a - lone, and

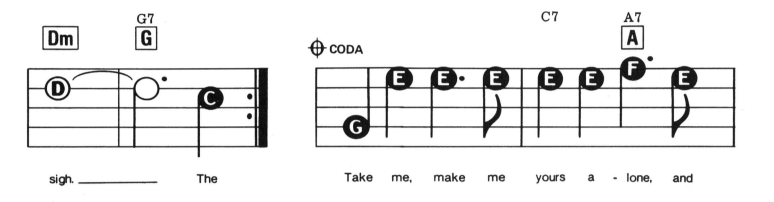

let the fu - ture be A - mong the gold - en

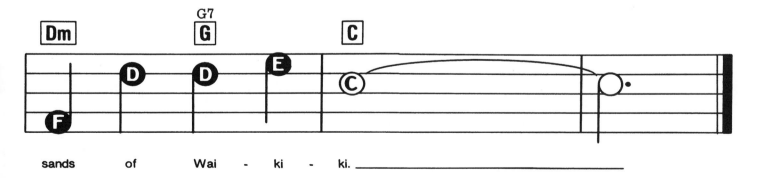

sands of Wai - ki - ki. _____

Sleepy Lagoon

Registration 1
Rhythm: Waltz

Words by Jack Lawrence
Music by Eric Coates

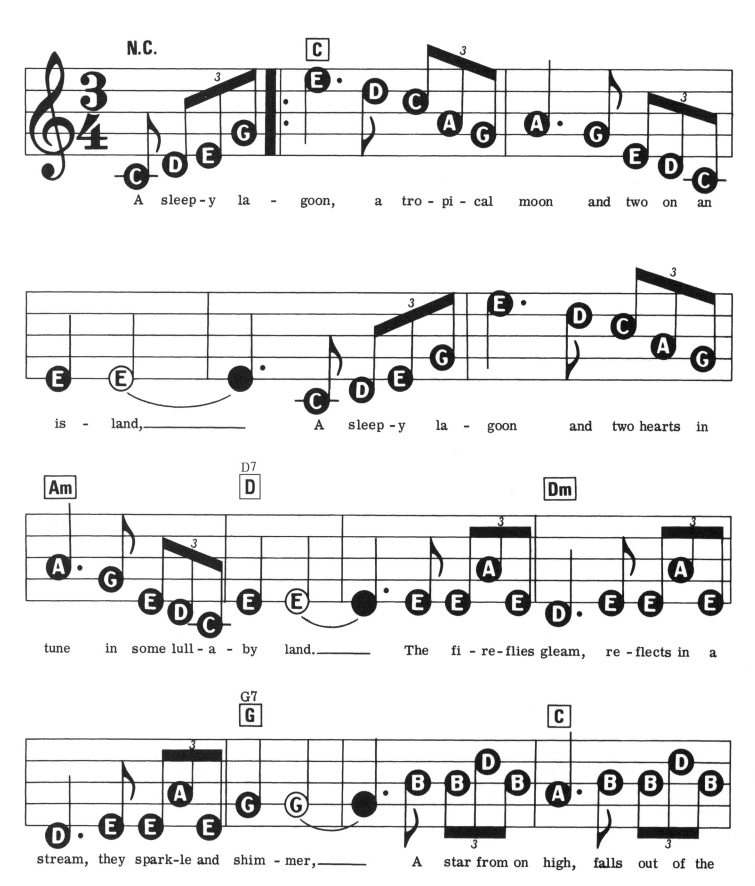

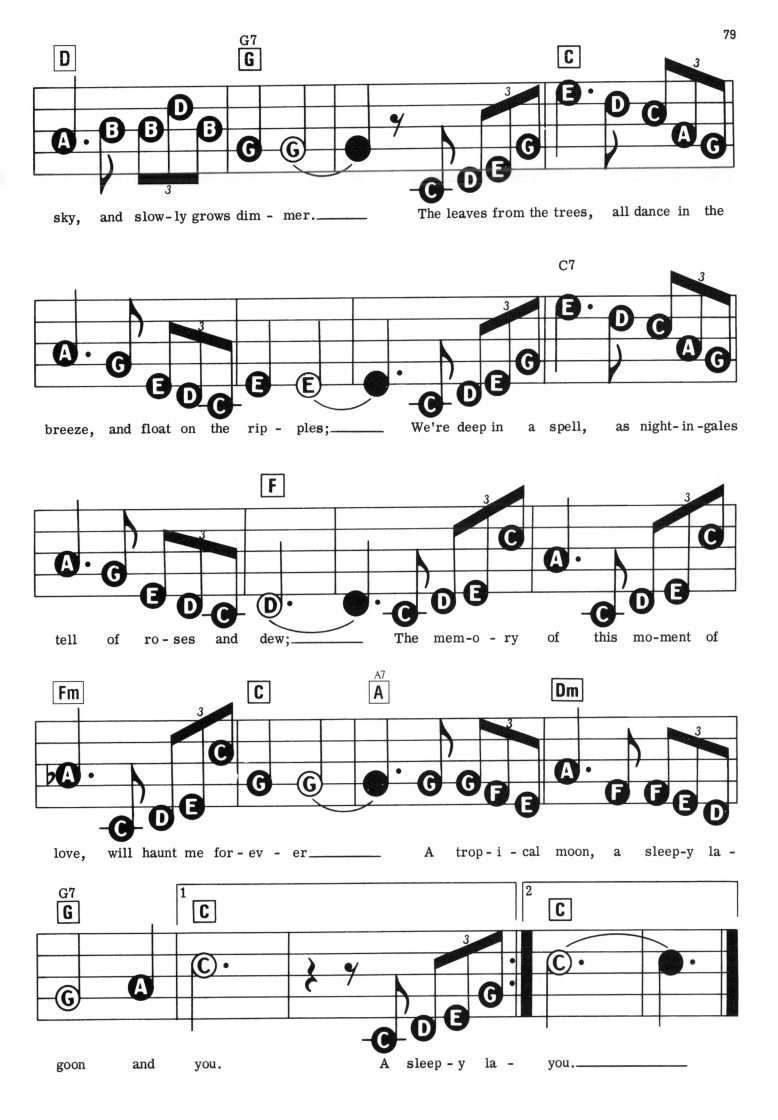

sky, and slow-ly grows dim - mer._____ The leaves from the trees, all dance in the

breeze, and float on the rip - ples;_____ We're deep in a spell, as night-in-gales

tell of ro - ses and dew;_____ The mem-o - ry of this mo-ment of

love, will haunt me for-ev - er_____ A trop-i - cal moon, a sleep-y la -

goon and you.   A sleep-y la - you._____

Song of the Islands

Registration 3
Rhythm: Fox Trot or Latin

Words and Music by
Charles E. King

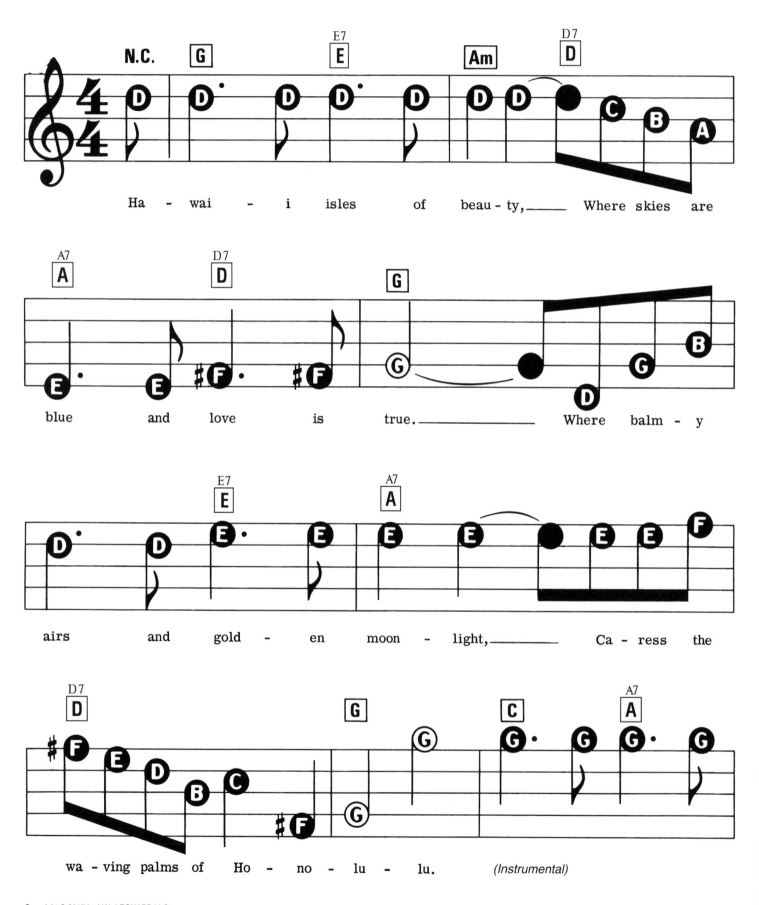

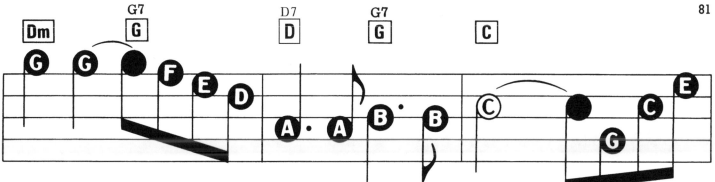

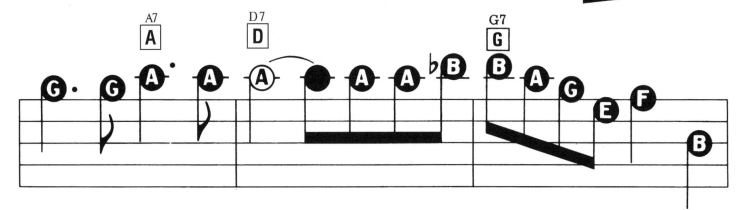

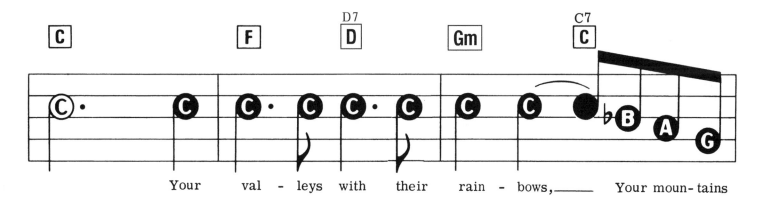

Your val - leys with their rain - bows,_____ Your moun-tains

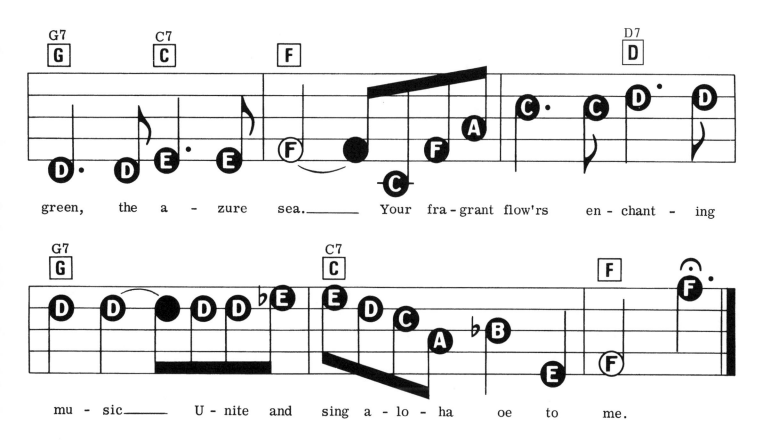

green, the a - zure sea._____ Your fra-grant flow'rs en - chant - ing

mu - sic_____ U - nite and sing a - lo - ha oe to me.

Sweet Leilani

Registration 4
Rhythm: Ballad or Swing

Words and Music by
Harry Owens

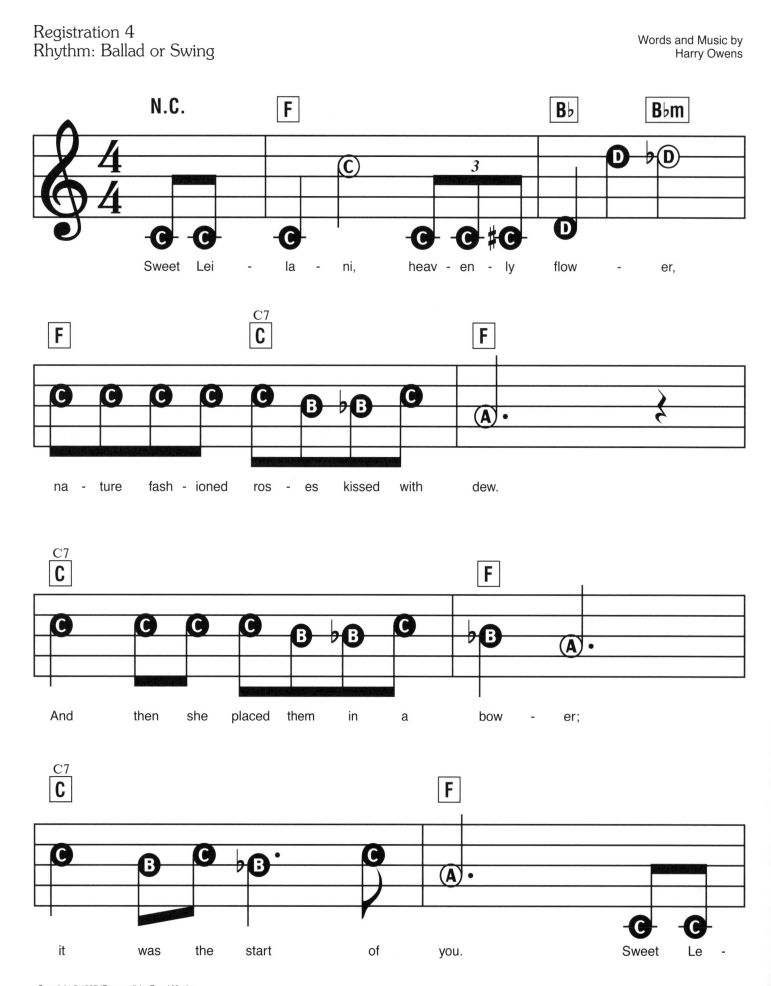

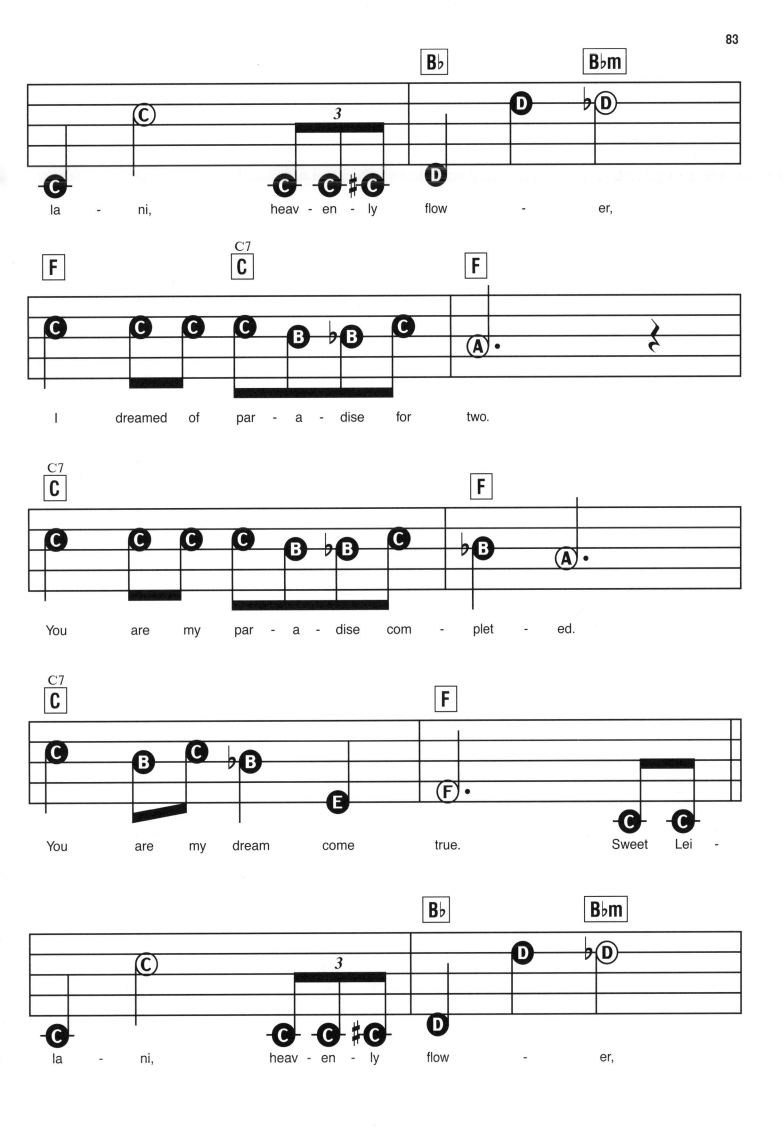

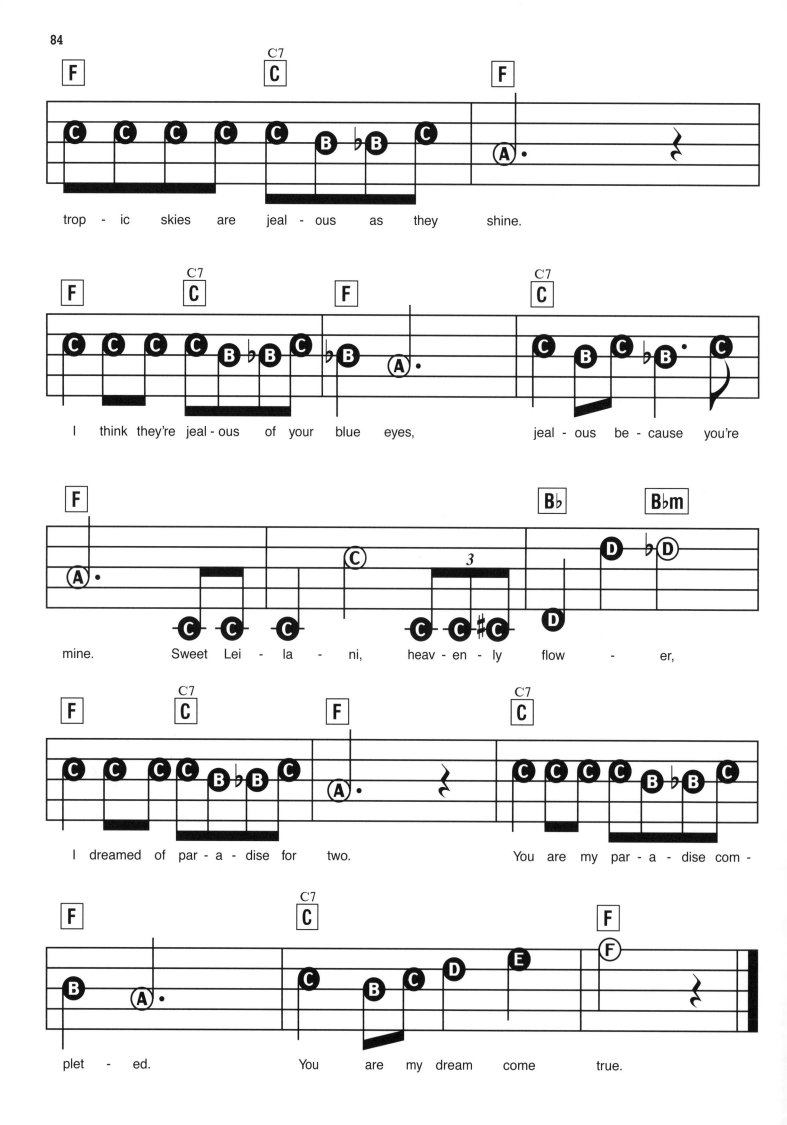

There's No Place Like Hawaii

Registration 8
Rhythm: Ballad or Fox Trot

Words and Music by Eddie Brandt
and Tony Todaro

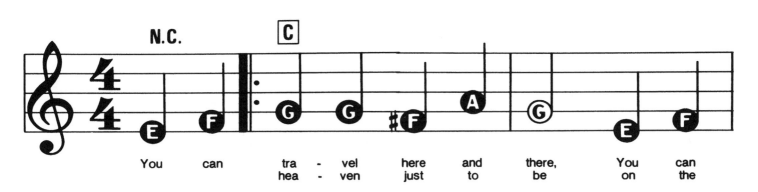

You can tra - vel here and there, You can
hea - ven here just and to be You on can the

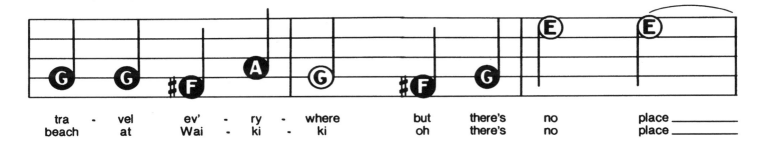

tra - vel ev' - ry - where but there's no place _____
beach at Wai - ki - ki oh there's no place _____

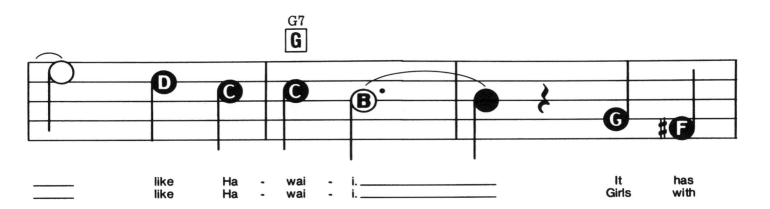

_____ like Ha - wai - i. _____ It has
_____ like Ha - wai - i. _____ Girls with

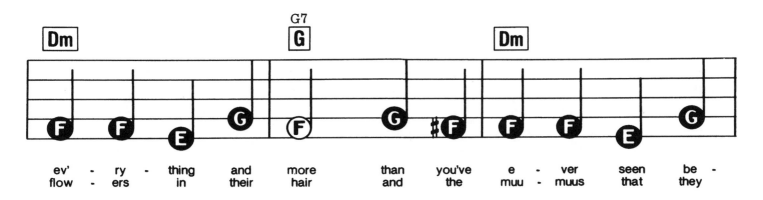

ev' - ry - thing and more than you've e - ver seen be -
flow - ers in their hair and the muu - muus that they

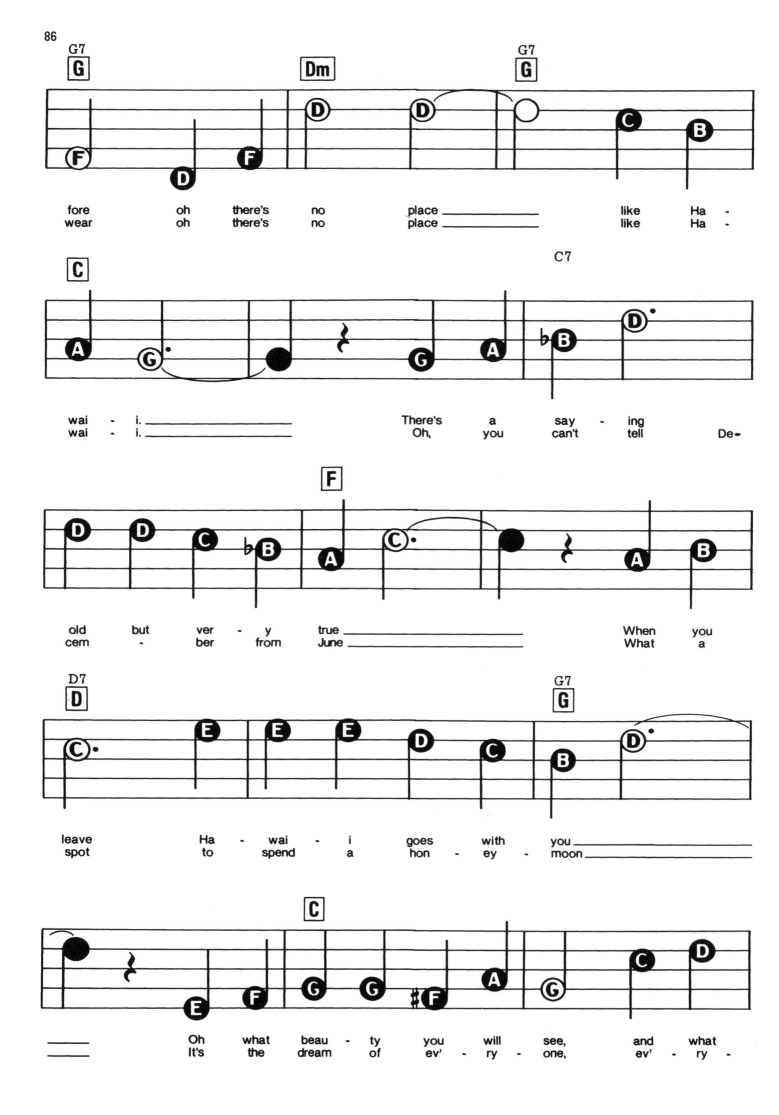

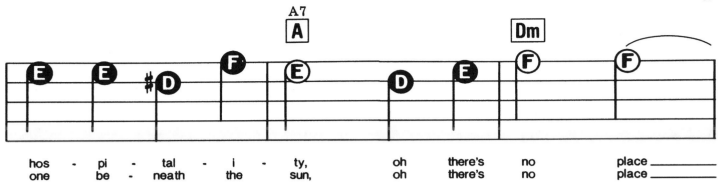

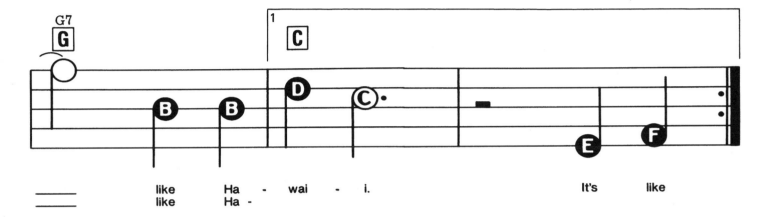

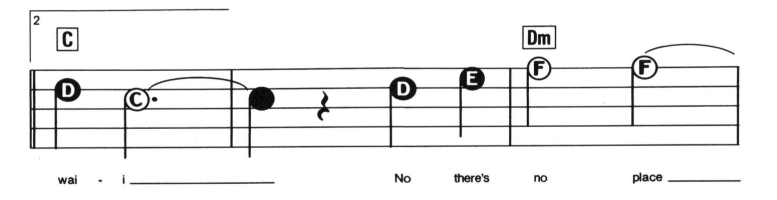

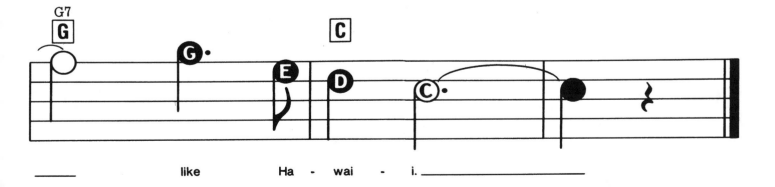

Sweet Someone

Registration 5
Rhythm: Latin or Swing

Words by George Waggner
Music by Baron Keyes

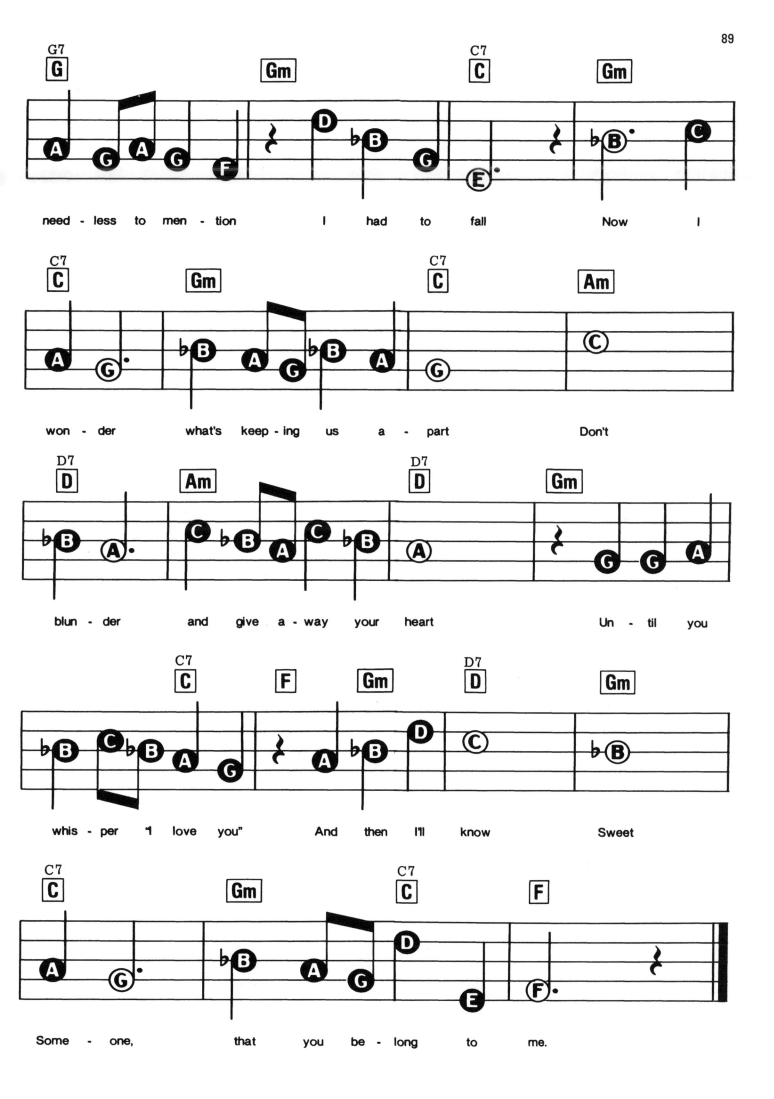

Tiny Bubbles

Registration 8
Rhythm: Slow Rock

Words and Music by
Leon Pober

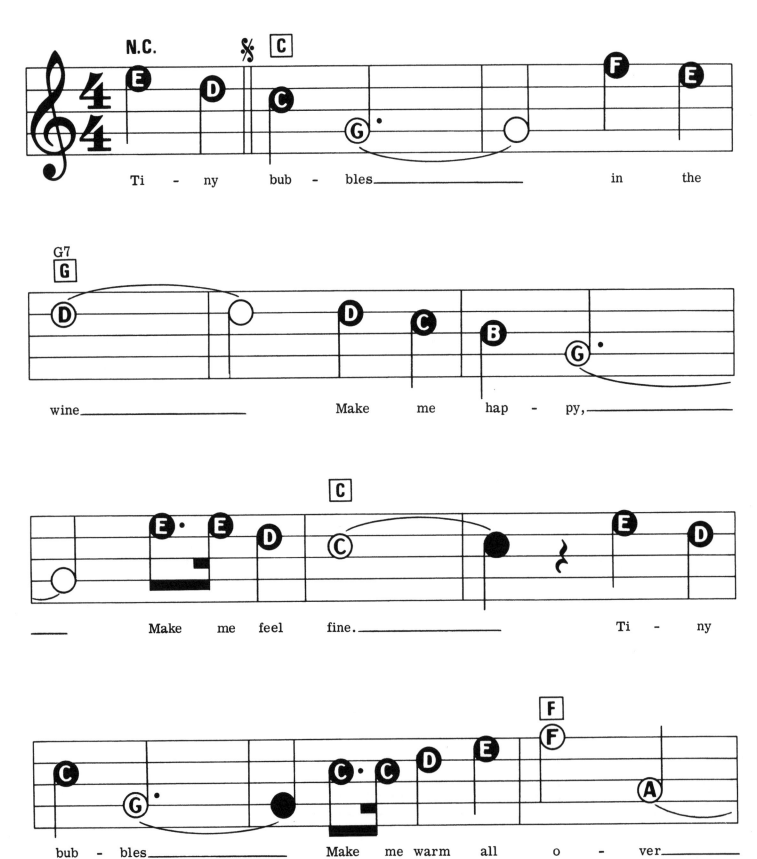

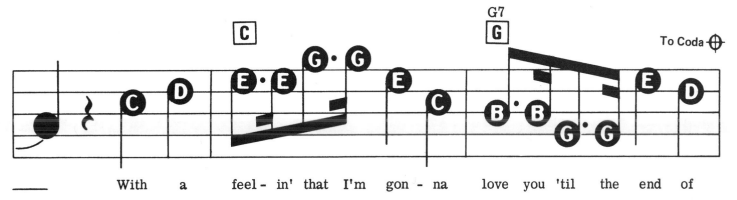

With a feel-in' that I'm gon-na love you 'til the end of

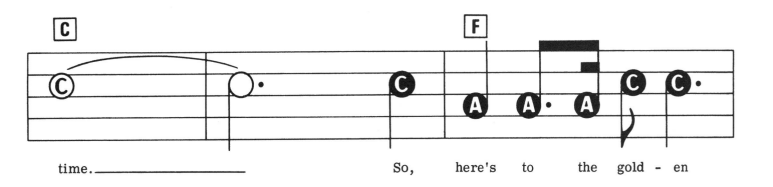

time._____ So, here's to the gold-en

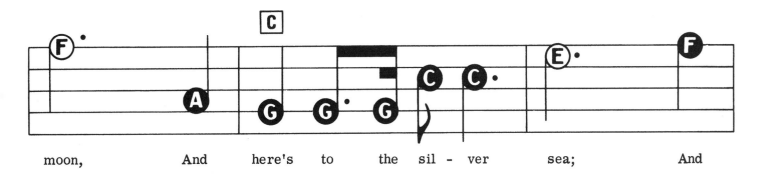

moon, And here's to the sil-ver sea; And

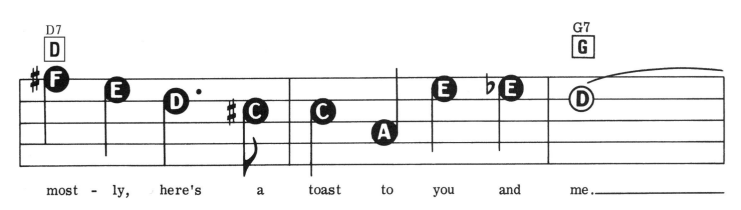

most-ly, here's a toast to you and me._____

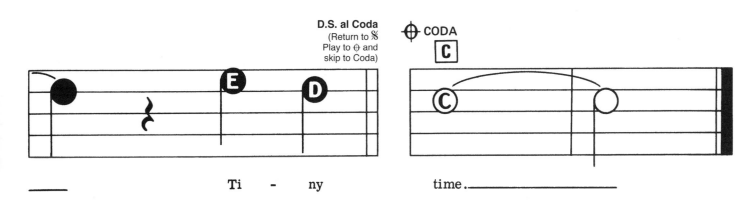

D.S. al Coda
(Return to %
Play to ⊕ and
skip to Coda)

⊕ **CODA**

Ti - ny

time._____

To You, Sweetheart, Aloha

Registration 4
Rhythm: Ballad or Fox Trot

Words and Music by
Harry Owens

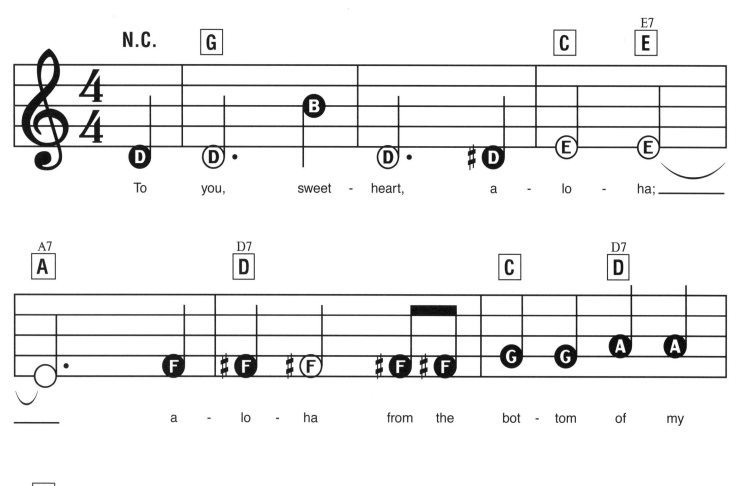

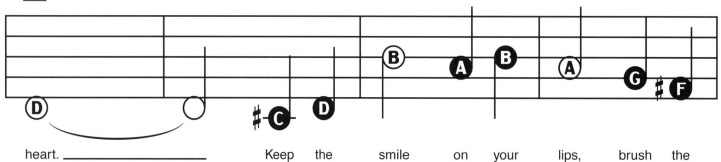

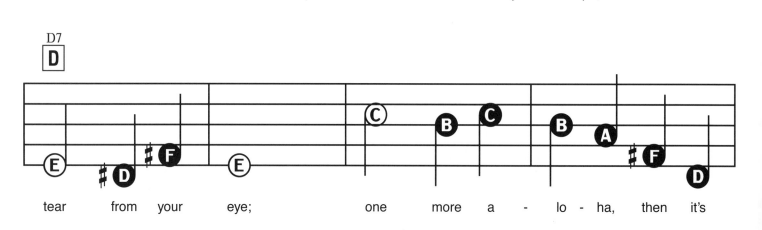

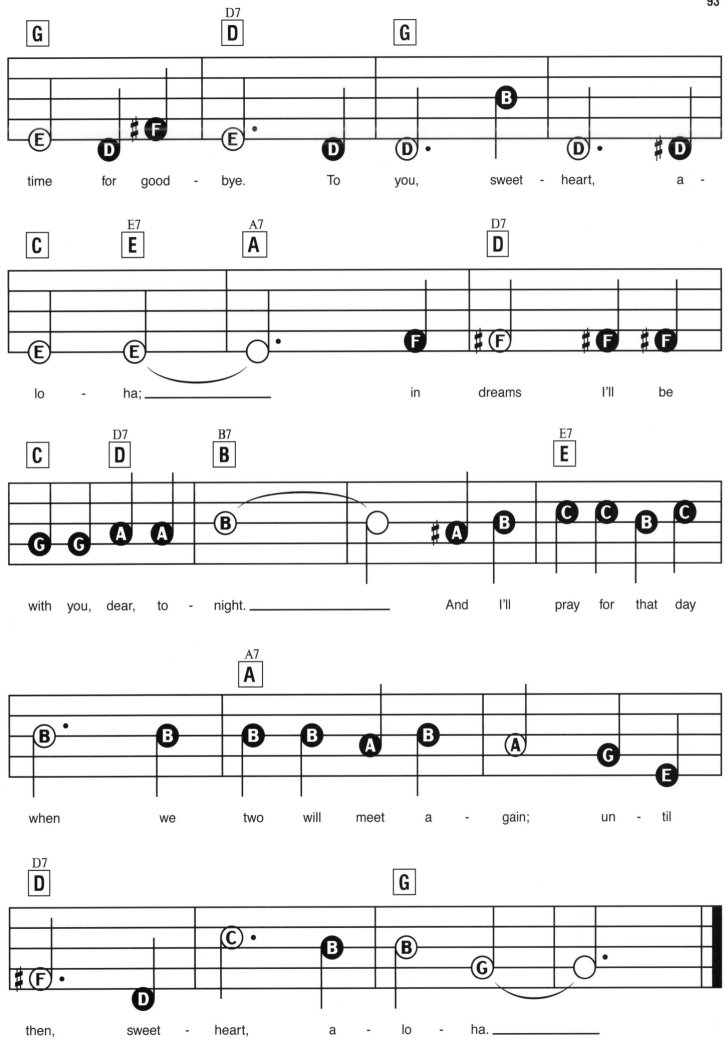

Waikiki

Registration 5
Rhythm: Ballad or Slow Rock

Words and Music by
Andy Cummings

Wai - ki - ki, At night when the sha - dows are
Wai - ki - ki, 'Tis for you that my heart is
Wai - ki - ki, My whole life is emp - ty with -

fall - ing, I hear your roll - ing surf call - ing,
yearn - ing, My thoughts are al - ways re - turn - ing,
out you, I miss that ma - gic a - bout you,

call - ing and call - ing to me.

Out there to you, a - cross the sea.

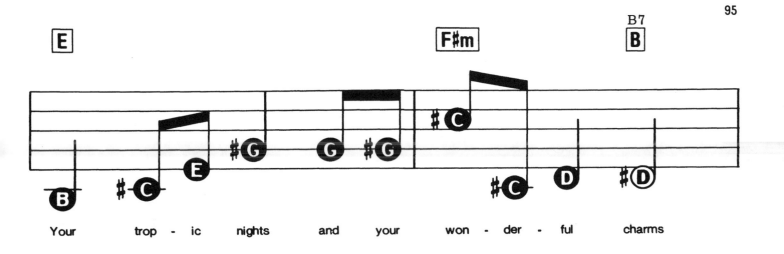

Your trop - ic nights and your won - der - ful charms

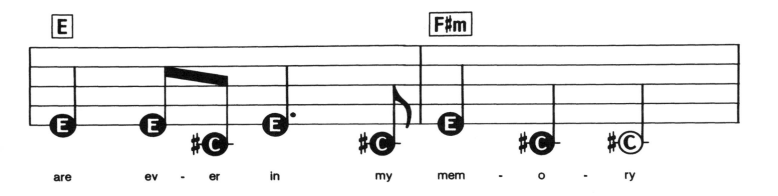

are ev - er in my mem - o - ry

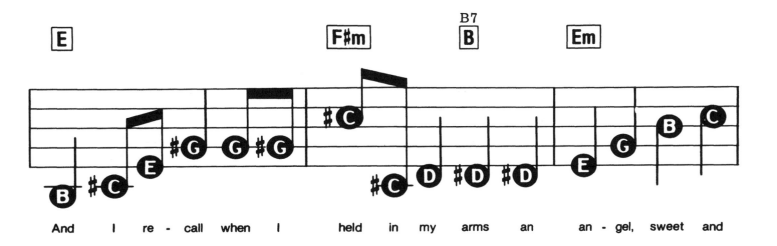

And I re - call when I held in my arms an an - gel, sweet and

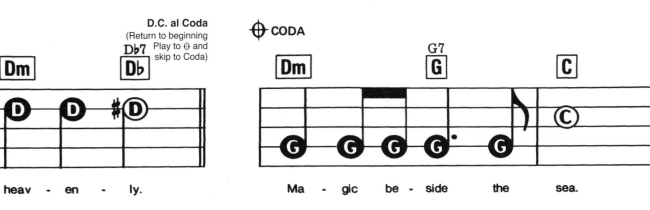

D.C. al Coda
(Return to beginning
Play to ⊕ and
skip to Coda)

⊕ **CODA**

heav - en - ly.

Ma - gic be - side the sea.

Yaaka Hula Hickey Dula

Registration 4
Rhythm: Swing

Words and Music by Ray Goetz,
Joe Young and Peter Wendling

G

D   #D   E ♭E   D

Down   Ha - wai - i   way,
Down   Ha - wai - i   way,
Down   Ha - wai - i   way,

D7 / D   G   D7 / D

B C B A   G

where I chance to stray,
by the moon - lit bay,
you would love to stay,

G   D7 / D

B A B A B   C•   A

on an eve - ning I   heard   a
when I lin - gered a   while,   she
if you'd ev - er see how   those

G7 / G   D7 / D

D D B A   G

hu - la maid - en play.
stole my heart a - way.
hu - las bend and sway.

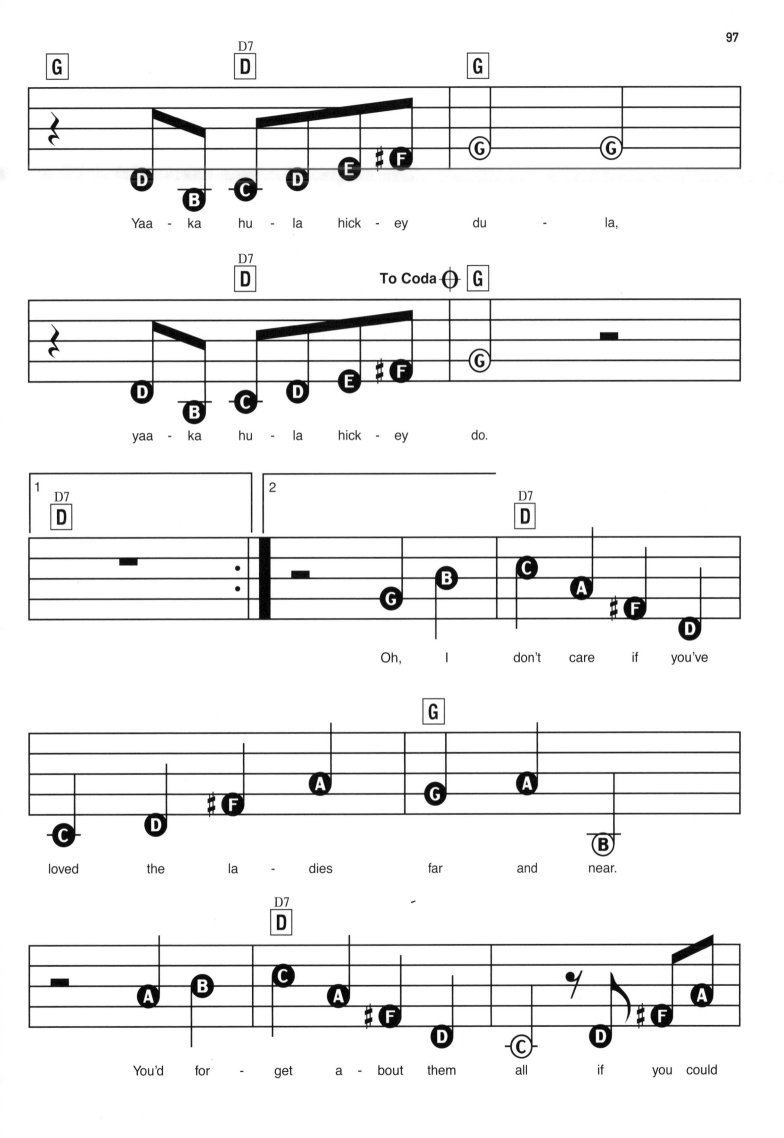

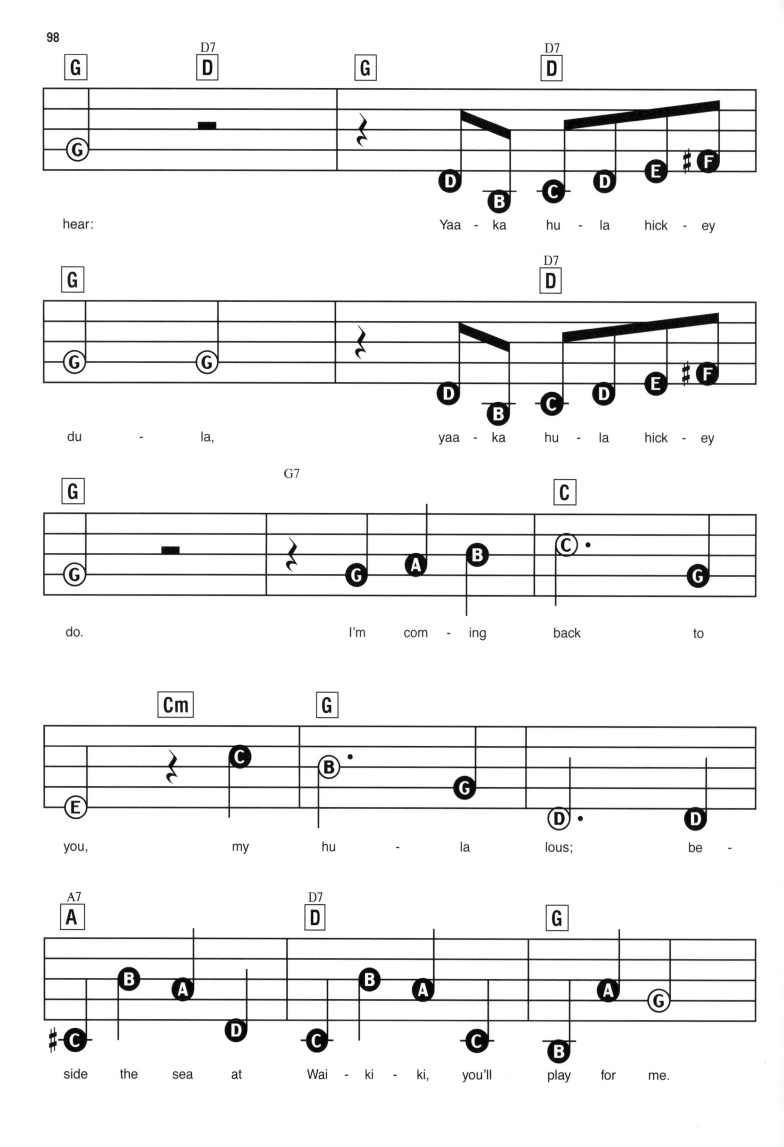

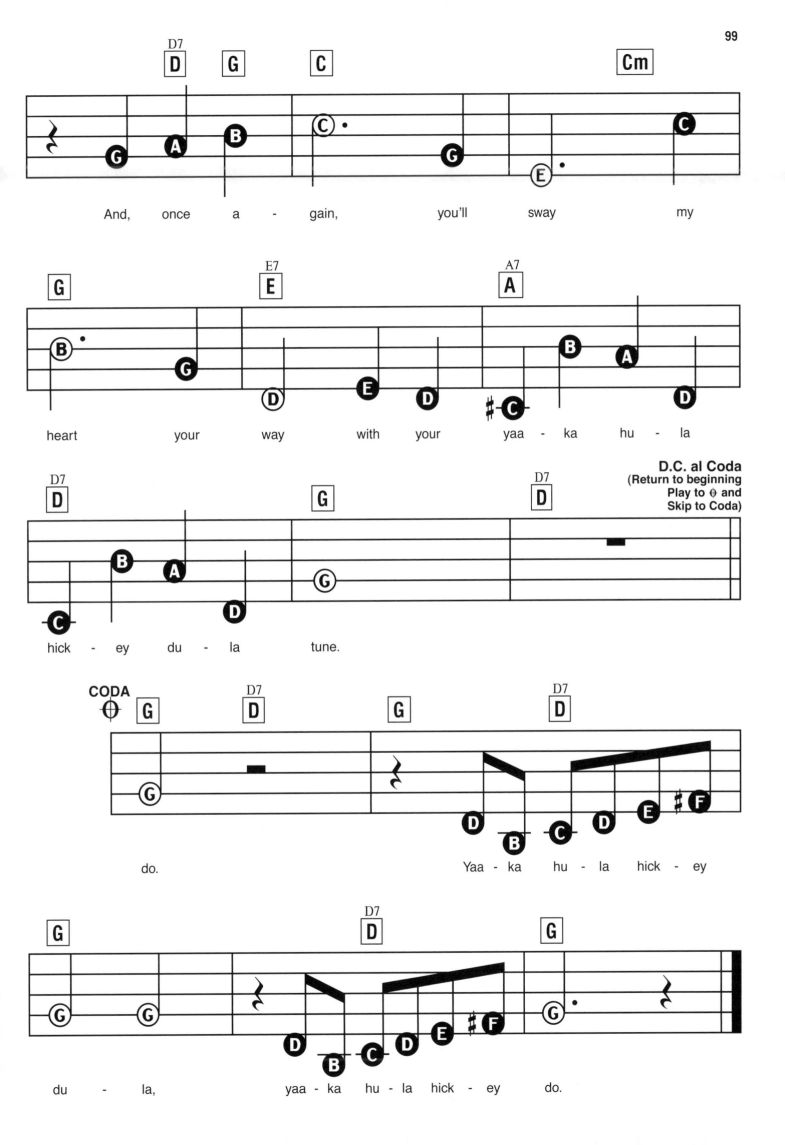

Ukulele Lady

Registration 4
Rhythm: Swing

Words by Gus Kahn
Music by Richard A. Whiting

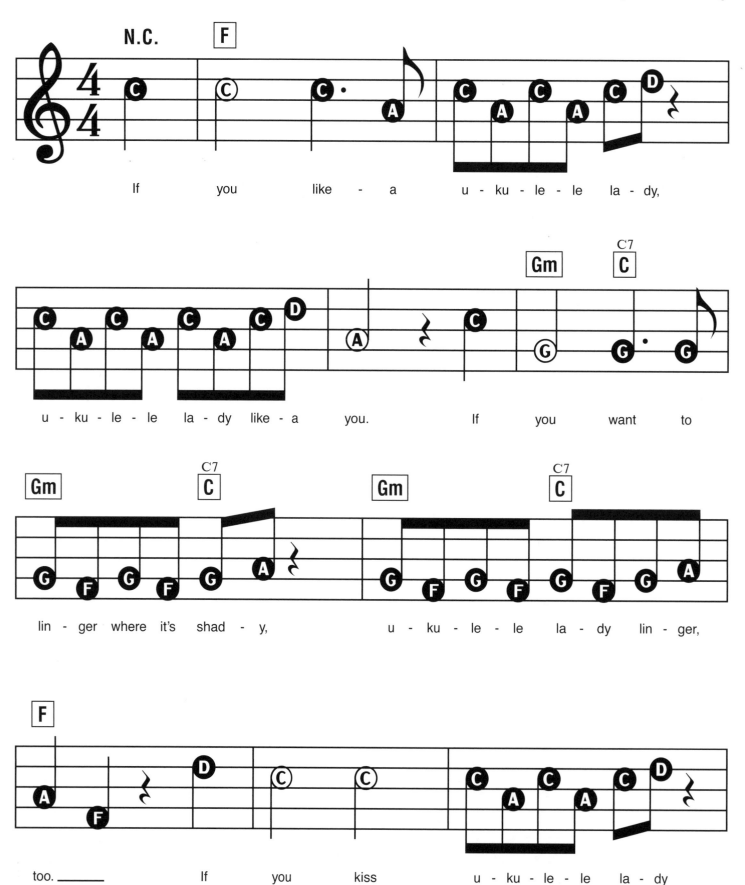

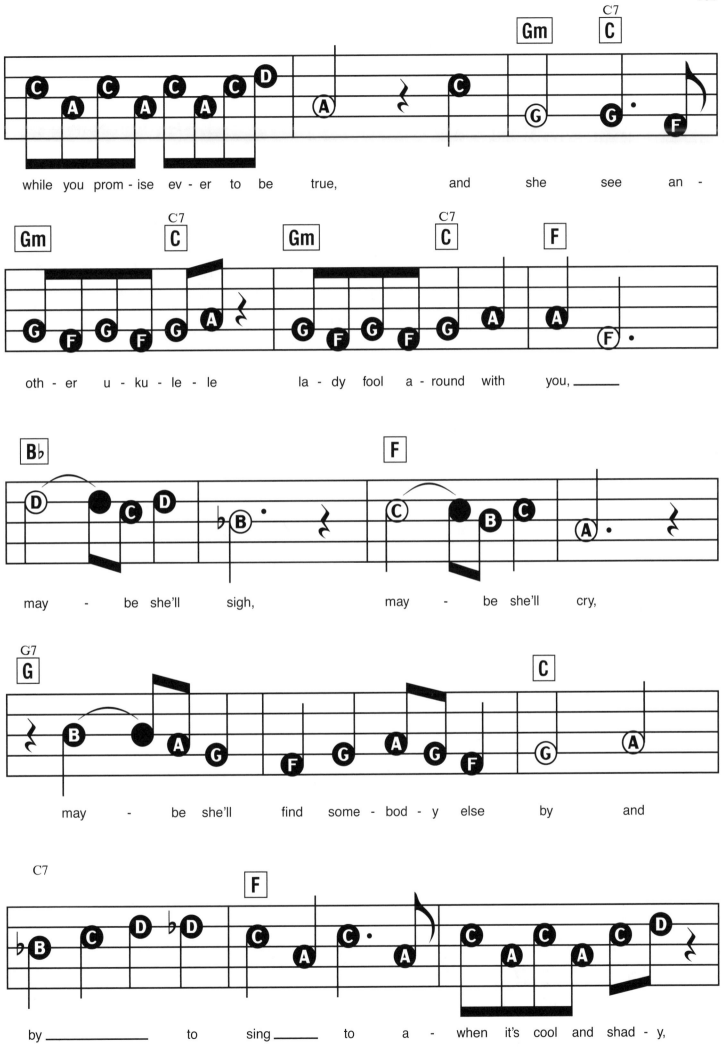

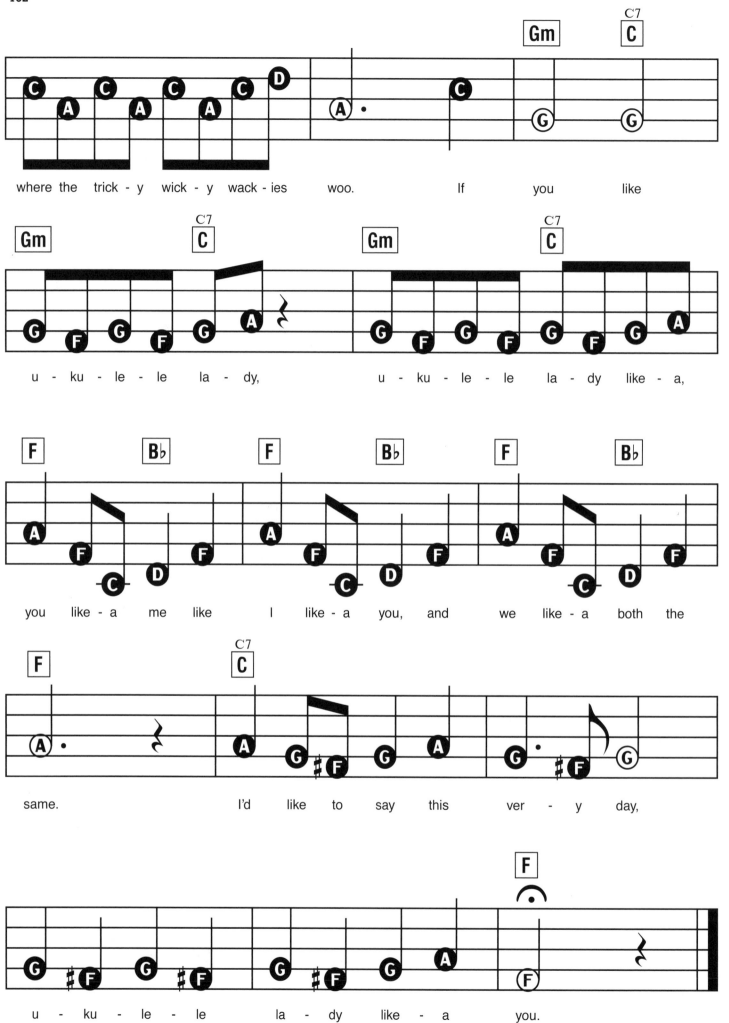

where the trick - y wick - y wack - ies woo. If you like

u - ku - le - le la - dy, u - ku - le - le la - dy like - a,

you like - a me like I like - a you, and we like - a both the

same. I'd like to say this ver - y day,

u - ku - le - le la - dy like - a you.

Registration Guide

- Match the Registration number on the song to the corresponding numbered category below. Select and activate an instrumental sound available on your instrument.

- Choose an automatic rhythm appropriate to the mood and style of the song. (Consult your Owner's Guide for proper operation of automatic rhythm features.)

- Adjust the tempo and volume controls to comfortable settings.

Registration

1	Mellow	Flutes, Clarinet, Oboe, Flugel Horn, Trombone, French Horn, Organ Flutes
2	Ensemble	Brass Section, Sax Section, Wind Ensemble, Full Organ, Theater Organ
3	Strings	Violin, Viola, Cello, Fiddle, String Ensemble, Pizzicato, Organ Strings
4	Guitars	Acoustic/Electric Guitars, Banjo, Mandolin, Dulcimer, Ukulele, Hawaiian Guitar
5	Mallets	Vibraphone, Marimba, Xylophone, Steel Drums, Bells, Celesta, Chimes
6	Liturgical	Pipe Organ, Hand Bells, Vocal Ensemble, Choir, Organ Flutes
7	Bright	Saxophones, Trumpet, Mute Trumpet, Synth Leads, Jazz/Gospel Organs
8	Piano	Piano, Electric Piano, Honky Tonk Piano, Harpsichord, Clavi
9	Novelty	Melodic Percussion, Wah Trumpet, Synth, Whistle, Kazoo, Perc. Organ
10	Bellows	Accordion, French Accordion, Mussette, Harmonica, Pump Organ, Bagpipes

00102278	1. Favorite Songs with 3 Chords	$7.99
00100374	2. Country Sound	$8.95
00100167	3. Contemporary Disney	$16.99
00100382	4. Dance Band Greats	$7.95
00100305	5. All-Time Standards	$7.99
00100428	6. Songs of The Beatles	$10.99
00100442	7. Hits from Musicals	$7.99
00100490	8. Patriotic Songs	$8.99
00100355	9. Christmas Time	$7.95
00100435	10. Hawaiian Songs	$7.95
00137580	11. 75 Light Classical Songs	$19.99
00110284	12. Star Wars	$9.99
00100248	13. Three-Chord Country Songs	$12.95
00100370	15. Country Pickin's	$7.95
00100335	16. Broadway's Best	$7.95
00100415	17. Fireside Singalong	$14.99
00149113	18. 30 Classical Masterworks	$8.99
00137780	19. Top Country Songs	$12.99
00102277	20. Hymns	$7.95
00197200	21. Good Ol' Gospel	$12.99
00100570	22. Sacred Sounds	$8.99
00140724	25. Happy Birthday to You and Other Great Songs	$10.99
14041364	26. Bob Dylan	$12.99
00001236	27. 60 of the World's Easiest to Play Songs with 3 Chords	$9.99
00101598	28. Fifty Classical Themes	$9.95
00100135	29. Love Songs	$9.99
00100030	30. Country Connection	$9.99
00100253	34. Inspirational Ballads	$10.95
00100122	36. Good Ol' Songs	$10.95
00100410	37. Favorite Latin Songs	$7.95
00156394	38. Best of Adele	$10.99
00159567	39. The Best Children's Songs Ever	$17.99
00119955	40. Coldplay	$10.99
00100123	42. Baby Boomers Songbook	$10.99
00100576	43. Sing-along Requests	$9.99
00102135	44. Best of Willie Nelson	$10.99
00156236	46. 15 Chart Hits	$12.99
00100007	47. Duke Ellington – American Composer	$8.95
00100343	48. Gospel Songs of Johnny Cash	$7.95
00102114	50. Best of Patsy Cline	$9.99
00100208	51. Essential Songs – The 1950s	$17.95
00100209	52. Essential Songs – The 1960s	$17.95
00100210	53. Essential Songs – The 1970s	$19.95
00100342	55. Johnny Cash	$10.99
00137703	56. Jersey Boys	$12.99
00100118	57. More of the Best Songs Ever	$17.99
00100285	58. Four-Chord Songs	$10.99
00100353	59. Christmas Songs	$10.99
00100304	60. Songs for All Occasions	$16.99
00102314	61. Jazz Standards	$10.95
00100409	62. Favorite Hymns	$6.95
00100360	63. Classical Music (Spanish/English)	$7.99
00100223	64. Wicked	$9.95
00100217	65. Hymns with 3 Chords	$7.99
00100218	67. Music from the Motion Picture Ray	$8.95
00100449	69. It's Gospel	$9.99
00100432	70. Gospel Greats	$7.95
00100117	72. Canciones Románticas	$7.99
00147049	74. Over the Rainbow & 40 More Great Songs	$12.99
00100568	75. Sacred Moments	$6.95
00100572	76. The Sound of Music	$9.99
00100424	81. Frankie Yankovic – Polkas & Waltzes	$7.95
00100286	87. 50 Worship Standards	$14.99
00100287	88. Glee	$9.99
00100577	89. Songs for Children	$7.95
00290104	90. Elton John Anthology	$16.99
00100034	91. 30 Songs for a Better World	$8.95
00100288	92. Michael Bublé – Crazy Love	$10.99
00100036	93. Country Hits	$12.99

00100139	94. Jim Croce – Greatest Hits	$9.99
00100219	95. The Phantom of the Opera (Movie)	$10.95
00100263	96. Mamma Mia – Movie Soundtrack	$7.99
00109768	98. Flower Power	$16.99
00119237	103. Two-Chord Songs	$9.99
00147057	104. Hallelujah & 40 More Great Songs	$12.99
00139940	106. 20 Top Hits	$12.99
00100256	107. The Best Praise & Worship Songs Ever	$16.99
00100363	108. Classical Themes (English/Spanish)	$6.95
00102232	109. Motown's Greatest Hits	$12.95
00101566	110. Neil Diamond Collection	$14.99
00100119	111. Season's Greetings	$15.99
00101498	112. Best of The Beatles	$19.99
00100134	113. Country Gospel USA	$12.99
00101612	115. The Greatest Waltzes	$9.99
00100136	118. 100 Kids' Songs	$12.95
00100433	120. Gospel of Bill & Gloria Gaither	$14.95
00100333	121. Boogies, Blues and Rags	$7.95
00100146	122. Songs for Praise & Worship	$8.95
00100001	125. Great Big Book of Children's Songs	$14.99
00101563	127. John Denver's Greatest Hits	$10.99
00116947	128. John Williams	$10.99
00140764	129. Campfire Songs	$10.99
00116956	130. Taylor Swift Hits	$10.99
00102318	131. Doo-Wop Songbook	$10.95
00100306	133. Carole King	$9.99
00001256	136. Christmas Is for Kids	$8.99
00100144	137. Children's Movie Hits	$7.95
00100038	138. Nostalgia Collection	$14.95
00100289	139. Crooners	$19.99
00101956	140. Best of George Strait	$12.95
00101946	143. The Songs of Paul McCartney	$8.99
00140768	144. Halloween	$10.99
00147061	147. Great Instrumentals	$9.99
00101548	150. Best Big Band Songs Ever	$16.95
00100152	151. Beach Boys – Greatest Hits	$9.99
00101592	152. Fiddler on the Roof	$9.99
00140981	153. Play Along with 50 Great Songs	$14.99
00101549	155. Best of Billy Joel	$12.99
00100315	160. The Grammy Awards Record of the Year 1958-2010	$16.99
00100293	161. Henry Mancini	$9.99
00100049	162. Lounge Music	$10.95
00100295	163. The Very Best of the Rat Pack	$12.99
00101530	164. Best Christmas Songbook	$9.99
00101895	165. Rodgers & Hammerstein Songbook	$9.95
00149300	166. The Best of Beethoven	$8.99
00149736	167. The Best of Bach	$8.99
00100148	169. A Charlie Brown Christmas™	$10.99
00101900	170. Kenny Rogers – Greatest Hits	$12.99
00101537	171. Best of Elton John	$9.99
00100321	173. Adele – 21	$12.99
00100149	176. Charlie Brown Collection™	$9.99
00102325	179. Love Songs of The Beatles	$10.99
00149881	180. The Best of Mozart	$8.99
00101610	181. Great American Country Songbook	$14.99
00001246	182. Amazing Grace	$12.99
00450133	183. West Side Story	$9.99
00100151	185. Carpenters	$10.99
00101606	186. 40 Pop & Rock Song Classics	$12.95
00100155	187. Ultimate Christmas	$18.99
00102276	189. Irish Favorites	$7.95
00100053	191. Jazz Love Songs	$8.95
00123123	193. Bruno Mars	$10.99
00124609	195. Opera Favorites	$8.99
00101609	196. Best of George Gershwin	$14.99
00100057	198. Songs in 3/4 Time	$9.95
00119857	199. Jumbo Songbook	$24.99
00101539	200. Best Songs Ever	$19.99
00101540	202. Best Country Songs Ever	$17.99

00101541	203. Best Broadway Songs Ever	$17.99
00101542	204. Best Easy Listening Songs Ever	$17.99
00101543	205. Best Love Songs Ever	$17.95
00100059	210. '60s Pop Rock Hits	$12.95
14041777	211. The Big Book of Nursery Rhymes & Children's Songs	$12.99
00126895	212. Frozen	$9.99
00101546	213. Disney Classics	$15.99
00101533	215. Best Christmas Songs Ever	$19.99
00131100	216. Frank Sinatra Centennial Songbook	$19.99
00100156	219. Christmas Songs with 3 Chords	$9.99
00102080	225. Lawrence Welk Songbook	$9.95
00101935	232. Songs of the '60s	$14.95
00101936	233. Songs of the '70s	$14.95
00101581	235. Elvis Presley Anthology	$15.99
00290170	239. Big Book of Children's Songs	$14.95
00100158	243. Oldies! Oldies! Oldies!	$10.95
00100041	245. Best of Simon & Garfunkel	$9.99
00100296	248. The Love Songs of Elton John	$12.99
00102113	251. Phantom of the Opera (Broadway)	$14.95
00100203	256. Very Best of Lionel Richie	$9.99
00100302	258. Four-Chord Worship	$9.99
00100178	259. Norah Jones – Come Away with Me	$10.99
00100063	266. Latin Hits	$7.95
00100062	269. Love That Latin Beat	$7.95
00101425	272. ABBA Gold – Greatest Hits	$9.99
00102248	275. Classical Hits – Bach, Beethoven & Brahms	$7.99
00100186	277. Stevie Wonder – Greatest Hits	$10.99
00100237	280. Dolly Parton	$9.99
00100068	283. Best Jazz Standards Ever	$15.95
00100244	287. Josh Groban	$14.99
00100022	288. Sing-a-Long Christmas	$12.99
00100023	289. Sing-a-Long Christmas Carols	$10.99
00102124	293. Movie Classics	$9.95
00100303	295. Best of Michael Bublé	$12.99
00100075	296. Best of Cole Porter	$7.95
00102130	298. Beautiful Love Songs	$7.95
00001102	301. Kid's Songfest	$10.99
00110416	302. More Kids' Songfest	$12.99
00102147	306. Irving Berlin Collection	$14.95
00102182	308. Greatest American Songbook	$9.99
00100194	309. 3-Chord Rock 'n' Roll	$8.95
02501515	312. Barbra – Love Is the Answer	$10.99
00100197	315. VH1's 100 Greatest Songs of Rock & Roll	$19.95
00100080	322. Dixieland	$7.95
00100277	325. Taylor Swift	$10.99
00100092	333. Great Gospel Favorites	$7.95
00100278	338. The Best Hymns Ever	$19.99
00100280	341. Anthology of Rock Songs	$19.99
00102235	346. Big Book of Christmas Songs	$14.95
00100095	359. 100 Years of Song	$17.95
00100096	360. More 100 Years of Song	$19.95
00159568	362. Songs of the 1920s	$19.99
00159569	363. Songs of the 1930s	$19.99
00159570	364. Songs of the 1940s	$19.99
00159571	365. Songs of the 1950s	$19.99
00159572	366. Songs of the 1960s	$19.99
00159573	367. Songs of the 1970s	$19.99
00159574	368. Songs of the 1980s	$19.99
00159575	369. Songs of the 1990s	$19.99
00100103	375. Songs of Bacharach & David	$7.95
00100107	392. Disney Favorites	$19.99
00100108	393. Italian Favorites	$7.95
00100111	394. Best Gospel Songs Ever	$17.95
00100114	398. Disney's Princess Collections	$12.99
00100115	400. Classical Masterpieces	$10.99

1016